Producer & International Distributor
eBookPro Publishing
www.ebook-pro.com

The Reform Haggadah

Copyright © 2024 MILAH TOVAH PRESS

All rights reserved; No parts of this book may be reproduced or transmitted in any form or by any means, electronic or mechanical, including photocopying, recording, taping, or by any information retrieval system, without the permission, in writing, of the author.

Cover & Illustrations: Maria Sokhatski
Editor: Dani Silas

Contact: agency@ebook-pro.com
ISBN **9789655754063**

Introduction

The festival of Passover is a joyous occasion for the Jewish people and an excellent opportunity to celebrate legacy and tradition with family and loved ones.

Reform Judaism shines a bright light of hope and progress upon the world, which is why this special Haggadah contains all the traditional Passover texts as well as commentary on the historical background of the rituals, discussions on modern issues of social justice, and a contemporary approach to a centuries-old tradition.

The English transliteration will always appear parallel to the original Hebrew text, with the English translation following below.

Also, icons alongside the text will help orient you and clarify what needs to be done next:

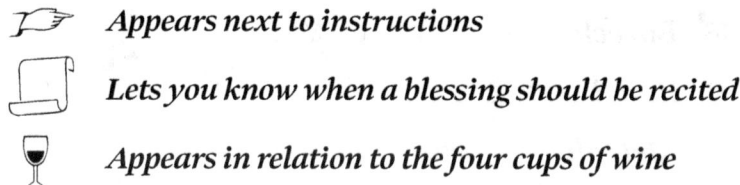

You can find all of your favorite Passover songs (Chad Gadya, Who Knows One?, Go Down Moses, Eliyahu Ha-Navi) all together in the Songs chapter, so you can skip back and forth and incorporate them in your Seder as you go along.

The Order of the Seder

7 **Kadesh** — Blessing on the Wine

15 **Urchatz** — Washing Hands

17 **Karpas** — The Leafy Vegetable

19 **Yachatz** — Breaking the Middle Matzah

21 **Magid** — Telling the Story of Exodus

57 **Rachtzah** — Washing Hands (this time, with a blessing)

59 **Motzi-Matzah** — Blessing on the Matzah

61 **Maror** — Bitter Herb

63 **Korech** — Maror Wrapped in Matzah

65 **Shulchan-Orech** — The Festive Meal

67 **Tzafun** — The Afikoman

69 **Barech** — Blessing After the Meal

73 **Hallel** — Praise to G-d

76 **Nirtzah** — Conclusion of the Seder

79 **Songs**

The Seder Plate

Maror
a bitter vegetable, usually horseradish or lettuce

Zero'a
typically a lamb shank bone, often substituted for cooked chicken

Beitzah
a hard-boiled egg

Charoset
a sweet paste made with apples and nuts

Karpas
a green leafy vegetable, usually parsley or celery

Hazeret
more of the same or a different bitter vegetable

Matzah
beside the seder plate, we place three whole matzahs, which will play an important part in the seder

Optional additions to the Seder Plate

In addition to the seven Passover symbols dictated by tradition, many choose to add foods to their Seder plate that hold more modern symbolism.

An orange – symbolizes LGBTQ+ awareness and equality. The orange represents marginalized members of the Jewish community and our complete acceptance of them within our society.

A banana – represents refugees. This important symbol shows that although we have a home to celebrate in, we do not forget the many misplaced men, women, and children caught up in their own modern-day Exodus.

Olives – symbolize peace. While there is nothing new about the connection between the olive branch and the symbol for peace, it is a progressive tradition to add some olives to the Seder Plate to express our hope for worldwide peace and stability.

Fair trade coffee or chocolate – for the people experiencing modern slavery. We may have left the land of Egypt and gained freedom from our slavery, but there are so many people and children still toiling in labor to provide for Western lifestyle. Choosing to include fair trade in your Passover celebration shows that you do not support the exploitation of some people for the luxuries of others.

You can decide which, if any, of these symbols mean something to you, your family, or your friends and add that to your Seder Plate to make it an even more meaningful occasion.

Kadesh

קַדֵּשׁ

Blessing on the Wine

Kadesh קַדֵּשׁ

Like things in Jewish tradition, the four cups of wine we drink during the Passover Seder are symbolic. They are said to symbolize the four actions promised to the Israelites by G-d in Exodus 6:

1. *"I will bring you out"*
2. *"I will deliver you"*
3. *"I will redeem you"*
4. *"I will take you in"*

Freedom, deliverance, redemption, and belonging. These four values are as important today as they were thousands of years ago, and the four cups of wine are here to remind us of that.

The Jewish people have historically fought against injustice and oppression of any kind, and continue to do so to this day. When we drink the four cups on Passover, we should remember to think of those people in need of freedom. Those in need of redemption, or deliverance, or simply to belong. They can be people in our lives or they can be far away from us, but they deserve our thoughts and prayers as we remember the time when our own people were saved from slavery, oppression, injustice, discrimination, overwork, and underpay.

🚩 *Pour everyone a first full cup of wine.*

Recite the Kiddush blessing, adding the parentheses when the Seder falls on the Sabbath:

וַיְהִי עֶרֶב וַיְהִי בֹקֶר יוֹם הַשִּׁשִּׁי וַיְכֻלּוּ הַשָּׁמַיִם וְהָאָרֶץ וְכָל צְבָאָם. וַיְכַל אֱלֹהִים בַּיּוֹם הַשְּׁבִיעִי מְלַאכְתּוֹ אֲשֶׁר עָשָׂה וַיִּשְׁבֹּת בַּיּוֹם הַשְּׁבִיעִי מִכָּל מְלַאכְתּוֹ אֲשֶׁר עָשָׂה. וַיְבָרֶךְ אֱלֹהִים אֶת יוֹם הַשְּׁבִיעִי וַיְקַדֵּשׁ אוֹתוֹ כִּי בוֹ שָׁבַת מִכָּל מְלַאכְתּוֹ אֲשֶׁר בָּרָא אֱלֹהִים לַעֲשׂוֹת.

Vayehi erev, vayehi voker, yom ha-shishi. V'yechulu ha-shamayim v'ha'aretz v'chol tzeva'am. V'yechal Elohim ba-yom ha-shevi'i mi-kol melachto asher asah, v'yishbot ba-yom ha-shvi'i mi-kol melachto asher asah. V'yevarech Elohim et yom ha-shvi'i v'yekadesh oto, ki vo shavat mi-kol melachto asher bara Elohim la'asot.

And so it was evening, and so it was morning, the sixth day. And G-d had completed the skies and the earth and all their host. And on the seventh day, G-d finished His work which He had done, and on the seventh day G-d rested from the work which He had done. And G-d blessed the seventh day and sanctified it, for on that day He rested from His work and all that He had done.

בָּרוּךְ אַתָּה יְיָ אֱלֹהֵינוּ מֶלֶךְ הָעוֹלָם בּוֹרֵא פְּרִי הַגָּפֶן.

Baruch atah Adonai, Eloheinu melech ha-olam, borei peri ha-gafen.

Blessed are You, Lord our G-d, King of the universe, creator of the fruit of the vine.

בָּרוּךְ אַתָּה יְיָ אֱלֹהֵינוּ מֶלֶךְ הָעוֹלָם, אֲשֶׁר בָּחַר בָּנוּ מִכָּל עָם וְרוֹמְמָנוּ מִכָּל לָשׁוֹן וְקִדְּשָׁנוּ בְּמִצְוֹתָיו. וַתִּתֶּן לָנוּ יְיָ אֱלֹהֵינוּ בְּאַהֲבָה (בְּשַׁבָּת: שַׁבָּתוֹת לִמְנוּחָה וּ) מוֹעֲדִים לְשִׂמְחָה, חַגִּים וּזְמַנִּים לְשָׂשׂוֹן, אֶת יוֹם (הַשַׁבָּת הַזֶּה וְאֶת יוֹם) חַג הַמַּצּוֹת הַזֶּה, זְמַן חֵרוּתֵנוּ (בְּאַהֲבָה), מִקְרָא קֹדֶשׁ, זֵכֶר לִיצִיאַת מִצְרָיִם. כִּי בָנוּ בָחַרְתָּ וְאוֹתָנוּ קִדַּשְׁתָּ מִכָּל הָעַמִּים, (וְשַׁבָּת) וּמוֹעֲדֵי קָדְשֶׁךָ (בְּאַהֲבָה וּבְרָצוֹן,) בְּשִׂמְחָה וּבְשָׂשׂוֹן הִנְחַלְתָּנוּ. בָּרוּךְ אַתָּה יְיָ, מְקַדֵּשׁ (הַשַׁבָּת וְ)יִשְׂרָאֵל וְהַזְּמַנִּים.

Baruch atah Adonai, Eloheinu melech ha-olam, asher bachar banu mi-kol 'am v'romema-nu mi-kol lashon v'kideshanu b'mitzvotav. V'titen lanu Adonai Eloheinu b'ahava (shabbatot li-mnucha v') mo'adim l'-simcha, chagim uzmanim l'sason, et yom (ha-shabbat hazeh ve'et yom) chag ha-matzot hazeh, zman cheruteinu (b'ahava) mikra kodesh, Zecher l'yetziyat mitzrayim. Ki banu bacharta v'otanu kidashta mi-kol ha-amim, (v'shabbat) umo'adei kodshecha (b'ahava uvratzon,) b'simcha uvsason hinchaltanu. Baruch atah Adonai, mekadesh (ha-shabbat v') Yisrael v'ha-zmanim.

Blessed are you, Lord our G-d, King of the universe, who has chosen us among all people and raised us above all languages, and sanctified us through His commandments. The Lord our G-d has lovingly given us (the Shabbat to rest, and) festivals to be joyful, holidays and special times for gladness, this (Shabbat day and

Kadesh

this) Passover, our time of (loving) freedom, in holiness and in memory of the Exodus from Egypt. For us You have chosen and us You have sanctified from all the people, and You have (lovingly and willingly) given us (Shabbat and) the holy times for happiness and joy. Blessed are You, G-d, who sanctifies (the Shabbat and) the people of Israel and the festivities.

Every week, when the sun sets on Saturday evening, we say "Havdalah" – Hebrew for "distinction." This is when we address the difference between the holy resting day of Shabbat and the remainder of the week. We thank G-d for differentiating between the holy and the mundane, light and dark, night and day, and between the people of Israel and the other nations of the world.

So, when Passover falls on Saturday evening, we add this shortened version of the Havdalah to the blessing on the wine:

On Saturday evening, add:

בָּרוּךְ אַתָּה יְיָ אֱלֹהֵינוּ מֶלֶךְ הָעוֹלָם,
בּוֹרֵא מְאוֹרֵי הָאֵשׁ.

Baruch atah Adonai, Eloheinu melech ha-olam, borei me'orei ha-esh.

Blessed are You, Lord our G-d, King of the universe, creator of the light of fire.

Kadesh

בָּרוּךְ אַתָּה יְיָ אֱלֹהֵינוּ מֶלֶךְ הָעוֹלָם הַמַּבְדִּיל בֵּין קֹדֶשׁ לְחֹל, בֵּין אוֹר לְחֹשֶׁךְ, בֵּין יִשְׂרָאֵל לָעַמִּים, בֵּין יוֹם הַשְּׁבִיעִי לְשֵׁשֶׁת יְמֵי הַמַּעֲשֶׂה. בֵּין קְדֻשַּׁת שַׁבָּת לִקְדֻשַּׁת יוֹם טוֹב הִבְדַּלְתָּ, וְאֶת יוֹם הַשְּׁבִיעִי מִשֵּׁשֶׁת יְמֵי הַמַּעֲשֶׂה קִדַּשְׁתָּ. הִבְדַּלְתָּ וְקִדַּשְׁתָּ אֶת עַמְּךָ יִשְׂרָאֵל בִּקְדֻשָּׁתֶךָ. בָּרוּךְ אַתָּה יְיָ הַמַּבְדִּיל בֵּין קֹדֶשׁ לְקֹדֶשׁ.

Baruch atah Adonai, Eloheinu melech ha-olam, ha-mavdil beyn kodesh le-chol, beyn or le-choshech, beyn Israel l'amim, beyn yom ha-shvi'i l'sheshet yemey ha-ma'aseh. Beyn kedushat shabbat l'kedushat yom tov hivdalta, v'et yom ha-shvi'i mi-sheshet yemey ha-ma'aseh kidashta. Hivdalta v'kidashta et amcha Yisrael b'kdushatcha. Baruch atah Adonai ha-mavdil beyn kodesh l'kodesh.

Blessed are You, Lord our G-d, King of the universe, who makes a distinction between the holy and the profane, between light and darkness, between the people of Israel and the nations, between the seventh day and the six days of work. You have made the distinction between the sanctity of Shabbat and the sanctity of the holy day, and sanctified the seventh day of the six days of work. You have set apart and sanctified Your people of Israel with Your holiness. Blessed are You, G-d, who differentiates between the holy and the holy.

As we go through the routine of life, we don't always stop to appreciate the wonderful privileges we have. We are blessed with a family and friends and people who love us, a home, hobbies, and everything we need.

Judaism is so special in that with its traditions, it reminds us every day to be thankful and grateful for all that we have. The value of gratitude is emphasized particularly in the very important and unique blessing, "Sh'hecheyanu" – the blessing of appreciation.

Sh'hecheyanu is special in that you can choose to say it whenever you please – to offer thanks for a new experience or blessing in your life. It is traditionally recited in events like the birth of a child, weddings, and the first night of Passover and other Jewish holidays. But you can choose to recite it for as small an occasion as wearing a new piece of clothing or sampling fruit you haven't tasted in a while.

That is the beauty of Sh'hecheyanu: it reminds us that any time and place is the right time and place to express our gratitude for the wonderful life we have been given.

 On the first Seder night, add:

בָּרוּךְ אַתָּה יְיָ אֱלֹהֵינוּ מֶלֶךְ הָעוֹלָם, שֶׁהֶחֱיָנוּ וְקִיְּמָנוּ וְהִגִּיעָנוּ לַזְּמַן הַזֶּה.

Baruch atah Adonai, Eloheinu melech ha-olam, sh'hecheyanu v'kiyemanu v'higiyanu l'zman hazeh.

Blessed are You, Lord our G-d, King of the universe, who has given us life, sustained us, and allowed us to reach this time.

 Drink the first cup of wine.

Urchatz

וּרְחַץ

Washing Hands

Urchatz וּרְחַץ

☞ *Wash your hands using a washing cup, pouring water three times onto each hand. Do not recite a blessing.*

Karpas

כַּרְפַּס

The Leafy Vegetable

Karpas כַּרְפַּס

"Karpas" means celery, but many choose to substitute it for any other fresh leafy vegetable, such as parsley, lettuce, scallions, cucumber, or even radish.

> *Take your leafy green vegetable and dip it into salt water.*

> *Recite the blessing:*

בָּרוּךְ אַתָּה יְיָ אֱלֹהֵינוּ מֶלֶךְ הָעוֹלָם, בּוֹרֵא פְּרִי הָאֲדָמָה.

Baruch atah Adonai, Eloheinu Melech ha-olam, borei peri ha-adama.

Blessed are You, Lord our G-d, King of the universe, creator of the fruit of the earth.

> *After reciting the blessing, eat the karpas.*

Yachatz

יַחַץ

Breaking the Middle Matzah

Yachatz יַחַץ

☞ Of the three matzahs we put aside at the start of the Seder, take the middle one and break it into two. Don't try to break it perfectly in half, as we want to have one piece bigger than the other.

☞ Take the larger piece and set it aside. This will be our Afikoman. It is customary for the leader of the seder to hide the Afikoman during the Seder for younger participants to find.

☞ Return the smaller piece to its place between the first and third matzahs.

Magid

מַגִּיד

Telling the Story
of Exodus

Magid מַגִּיד

 Uncover the Matzah for all to see, and raise it in the air while reciting the following:

הָא לַחְמָא עַנְיָא דִּי אֲכָלוּ אַבְהָתָנָא בְּאַרְעָא דְמִצְרָיִם. כָּל דִּכְפִין יֵיתֵי וְיֵיכֹל, כָּל דִּצְרִיךְ יֵיתֵי וְיִפְסַח. הָשַׁתָּא הָכָא, לְשָׁנָה הַבָּאָה בְּאַרְעָא דְיִשְׂרָאֵל. הָשַׁתָּא עַבְדֵי, לְשָׁנָה הַבָּאָה בְּנֵי חוֹרִין.

Ha lachma anya, di achalu avhatana b'ar'a d'mitsrayim. Kol dichfin yetey v'yechol, kol ditsrich yetey v'yifsach. Hashata hacha, l'shana haba'a b'ara d'yisrael. Hashata avdey, l'shana haba'a bney chorin.

This is the bread of poverty that our ancestors ate in the land of Egypt. All who are hungry may come and eat, all who are in need may come and celebrate with us. Now we are here, here's to next year in the land of Israel. Now we are slaves, here's to next year as a free people.

 Put the matzah down and cover it again.

 Pour the second cup of wine.

Mah Nishtanah – What Is Different?

☞ *It is traditional for the youngest participant of each Seder to ask the four questions, with the rest of the participants replying.*

מַה נִּשְׁתַּנָּה הַלַּיְלָה הַזֶּה מִכָּל הַלֵּילוֹת ?	Mah nishtanah halaylah hazeh mikol haleylot?
שֶׁבְּכָל הַלֵּילוֹת אָנוּ אוֹכְלִין חָמֵץ וּמַצָּה, הַלַּיְלָה הַזֶּה - כֻּלּוֹ מַצָּה.	She-b'kol haleylot anu ochlin chametz u'matzah, halaylah hazeh – kulo matzah.
שֶׁבְּכָל הַלֵּילוֹת אָנוּ אוֹכְלִין שְׁאָר יְרָקוֹת, - הַלַּיְלָה הַזֶּה מָרוֹר.	She-b'kol haleylot anu ochlin she'ar yerakot, halaylah hazeh – maror.
שֶׁבְּכָל הַלֵּילוֹת אֵין אָנוּ מַטְבִּילִין אֲפִילוּ פַּעַם אֶחָת, - הַלַּיְלָה הַזֶּה שְׁתֵּי פְעָמִים.	She-b'kol haleylot eynanu matbilin afilu pa'am achat, halaylah hazeh – shtey pe'amim.
שֶׁבְּכָל הַלֵּילוֹת אָנוּ אוֹכְלִין בֵּין יוֹשְׁבִין וּבֵין מְסֻבִּין, - הַלַּיְלָה הַזֶּה כֻּלָּנוּ מְסֻבִּין.	She-b'kol haleylot anu ochlin beyn yoshvin u'beyn mesubin, halaylah hazeh – kulanu mesubin.

What makes this night different from any other night?
On every other night we eat chametz and matzah. On this night – only matzah.
On every other night we eat all kinds of vegetables. On this night – only maror.
On every other night we do not dip our vegetables even once. On this night – we dip twice.
On every other night we eat reclining and sitting straight. On this night – we all recline.

On this special night, Judaism tells us to take a break and a hard look at how we see the things around us. We don't just let this evening pass like any other, but we make sure that even the youngest kid at the table is able to ask questions, to express interest in what goes on around them. This is a reminder to us not to go through life simply accepting what we've always known to be true. Social prejudice, racism, sexism, gender inequality, and many realities that have no place in today's world are all caused by people being unable to see things in a new light.

However, when we are socially aware and question what we know from a very young age, we open ourselves up to become more accepting, educated people.

עֲבָדִים הָיִינוּ לְפַרְעֹה בְּמִצְרָיִם, וַיּוֹצִיאֵנוּ יְיָ אֱלֹהֵינוּ מִשָּׁם בְּיָד חֲזָקָה וּבִזְרוֹעַ נְטוּיָה. וְאִלּוּ לֹא הוֹצִיא הַקָּדוֹשׁ בָּרוּךְ הוּא אֶת אֲבוֹתֵינוּ מִמִּצְרַיִם, הֲרֵי אָנוּ וּבָנֵינוּ וּבְנֵי בָנֵינוּ מְשֻׁעְבָּדִים הָיִינוּ לְפַרְעֹה בְּמִצְרָיִם.

Avadim hayinu l'paroh b'mitsrayim, v'yotsi'anu Adonai Eloheinu misham b'yad chazakah u'vizro'a netuya. V'ilu lo hotzi ha-Kadosh Baruch Hu et avoteynu m'mitsrayim, harey anu u'vaneynu u'vney vaneynu meshu'abadim hayinu l'paroh b'mitsrayim

We were slaves of Pharoah in Egypt, until the Lord our G-d took us out from there with a strong hand and an outstretched arm. Had G-d, blessed be His name, not liberated our ancestors from Egypt, we and our sons and daughters and their sons and daughters would still be enslaved to Pharoah in Egypt today.

Magid

אֲפִילוּ כֻּלָּנוּ חֲכָמִים, כֻּלָּנוּ נְבוֹנִים, כֻּלָּנוּ זְקֵנִים, כֻּלָּנוּ יוֹדְעִים אֶת הַתּוֹרָה, מִצְוָה עָלֵינוּ לְסַפֵּר בִּיצִיאַת מִצְרָיִם. וְכָל הַמַּרְבֶּה לְסַפֵּר בִּיצִיאַת מִצְרַיִם הֲרֵי זֶה מְשֻׁבָּח.

V'afilu kulanu chachamim, kulanu nevonim, kulanu zkenim, kulanu yod'im et ha-torah, mitzvah aleynu lesaper b'yetsiat mitsrayim. V'chol hamarbeh lesaper b'yetsiat mitsrayim, harey zeh meshubach.

And although we are all intelligent, wise, learned, we all know the torah, we are commanded to tell the story of the Exodus from Egypt. And the more we tell the story, the better.

מַעֲשֶׂה בְּרַבִּי אֱלִיעֶזֶר וְרַבִּי יְהוֹשֻׁעַ וְרַבִּי אֶלְעָזָר בֶּן עֲזַרְיָה וְרַבִּי עֲקִיבָא וְרַבִּי טַרְפוֹן שֶׁהָיוּ מְסֻבִּין בִּבְנֵי בְרַק, וְהָיוּ מְסַפְּרִים בִּיצִיאַת מִצְרַיִם כָּל אוֹתוֹ הַלַּיְלָה עַד שֶׁבָּאוּ תַלְמִידֵיהֶם וְאָמְרוּ לָהֶם: רַבּוֹתֵינוּ, הִגִּיעַ זְמַן קְרִיאַת שְׁמַע שֶׁל שַׁחֲרִית.

Ma'aseh b'rabi Eliezer v'rabi Yehoshua v'rabi Elazar ben azaryah v'rabi akiva v'rabi tardon she-hayu mesubin bivney beraq, v'hayu mesaprim b'yetzi'at mitzrayim kol oto ha'laylah ad she-ba'u talmideyhem v'amru lahem: raboteynu, higiya zeman kriyat shema shel shacharit.

A story is told of Rabbi Eliezer and Rabbi Yehoshua and Rabbi Elazar Ben Azaryah and Rabbi Akiva and Rabbk Tarfon, who resided in Benei Beraq, and told the story of the exodus from Egypt all that night. Until their students came to them and told them: our teachers, it is time to say the shema for the morning prayer

אָמַר רַבִּי אֶלְעָזָר בֶּן עֲזַרְיָה: הֲרֵי אֲנִי כְּבֶן שִׁבְעִים שָׁנָה, וְלֹא זָכִיתִי שֶׁתֵּאָמֵר יְצִיאַת מִצְרַיִם בַּלֵּילוֹת עַד שֶׁדְּרָשָׁהּ בֶּן זוֹמָא: שֶׁנֶּאֱמַר, לְמַעַן תִּזְכֹּר אֶת יוֹם צֵאתְךָ מֵאֶרֶץ מִצְרַיִם כֹּל יְמֵי חַיֶּיךָ, יְמֵי חַיֶּיךָ - הַיָּמִים, כָּל יְמֵי חַיֶּיךָ - הַלֵּילוֹת. וַחֲכָמִים אוֹמְרִים: יְמֵי חַיֶּיךָ - הָעוֹלָם הַזֶּה, כֹּל יְמֵי חַיֶּיךָ - לְהָבִיא לִימוֹת הַמָּשִׁיחַ.

Amar rabi Elazar ben Azaryah: herey ani k'ven shivim shanah, v'lo zachiti she-teyamer yetzi'at mitzrayim ba'leylot ad she'drashah ben zoma: she-ne'eymar, l'ma'an tizkor et yom tzeytcha m'eretz mitzrayim kol yemey chayeycha, yemey chayeych – ha-yamim, kol yemey chayeych – ha-leylot. V'chachamim omrim: yemey chayeycha – ha-olam hazeh, kol yemey chayeycha – l'havi l'yimot ha-mashiyach.

Rabbi Elazar Ben Azaryah would say: I am seventy years old and I have not been privileged to hear the story of the exodus from Egypt being told at night. Until Ben Zoma declared: It is said, you must remember the day you were delivered from Egypt for all the days of your life. The days of your life – the days. All the days of your life – the nights. And the sages say, the days of your life – this world. All the days of your life – the days of the Messiah.

בָּרוּךְ הַמָּקוֹם, בָּרוּךְ הוּא. בָּרוּךְ שֶׁנָּתַן תּוֹרָה לְעַמּוֹ יִשְׂרָאֵל, בָּרוּךְ הוּא.

Baruch ha-makom, baruch hu. Baruch she-natan torah l'amo Yisrael, baruch hu.

Blessed is G-d, blessed is He. Blessed is He who gave the Torah to the people of Israel, blessed is He.

The Torah is the foundation upon which the entire Jewish culture and tradition is built. While its source, human or divine, is contested, it remains a solid base for the orthodox Jewish lifestyle.

Reform Judaism takes the Torah one step further, treating the scriptures as an important but *adaptable* guideline, which can and should change to reflect modern thinking.

That is why it is so important that people continue to study and question the teachings of Judaism, ensuring that we are progressing along with the modern world and not falling behind to archaic traditions and thought.

The Four Children

כְּנֶגֶד אַרְבָּעָה בָנִים דִּבְּרָה תוֹרָה. אֶחָד חָכָם, וְאֶחָד רָשָׁע, וְאֶחָד תָּם, וְאֶחָד שֶׁאֵינוֹ יוֹדֵעַ לִשְׁאוֹל.

Ke-neged arba'ah banim dibrah torah. Echad chacham, v'echad rasha, v'echad tam, v'eched she'eyno yode'a lishol.

The Torah tells us of four children. One who is wise, one who is wicked, one who is simple, and one who does not know how to ask.

Magid

The wise child is inquisitive, curious, and willing to learn. They want to know all about the traditions of Passover and discover their roots.

To the wise child, you shall respond with the detailed story of Passover and the many intricate rules and laws of the festival.

The wicked children separate themselves from their community. They do not see themselves as Jews or as a part of the Jewish nation, rather they view Passover as if watching it from the sidelines.

For these children, we must find unique ways to engage them in the holiday and its traditions. Do not simply give up on them, but show them the advantages and privileges of belonging to a group or community so that they do feel included and not left out.

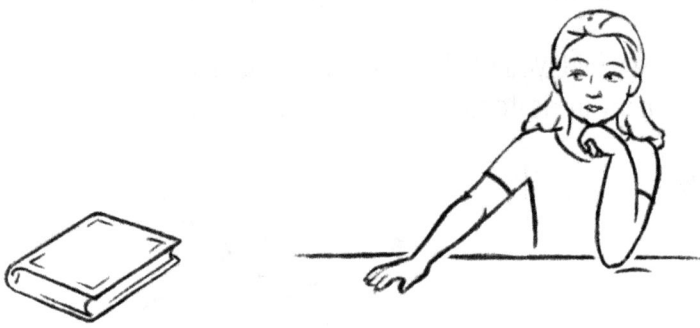

The simple children are interested, but not quite advanced enough to understand the complexities of the Jewish holiday. All they can ask is, what's all this?

Our duty is to tell them the wonderful story of Passover in clear, simple language that they will understand and relate to.

And the children who are too young or simple to ask, you shall tell them the story yourself. Make sure to include even the youngest children, and allow them to share in their legacy and heritage as true members of the Jewish community.

Magid

וְהִגַּדְתָּ לְבִנְךָ - יָכוֹל מֵרֹאשׁ חֹדֶשׁ? תַּלְמוּד לוֹמַר: בַּיּוֹם הַהוּא; אִי בַּיּוֹם הַהוּא, יָכוֹל מִבְּעוֹד יוֹם? תַּלְמוּד לוֹמַר: בַּעֲבוּר זֶה - בַּעֲבוּר זֶה לֹא אָמַרְתִּי, אֶלָּא בְּשָׁעָה שֶׁיֵּשׁ מַצָּה וּמָרוֹר מֻנָּחִים לְפָנֶיךָ.

V'higadeta l'vincha – yachol m'rosh chodesh? Talmud lomar: ba-yom hahu; I ba-yom hahu, yachol mi-be'od yom? Talmud lomar: ba'avur zeh lo amarti, ela b'sha'ah she-yesh matzah u'maror munachim lefaneycha.

And you shall tell him the story yourself – one might think that you must tell the story from the start of the month. The Torah says: on that day. Can "that day" mean before nightfall? The Torah says: only when the matzah and maror are laid before you.

מִתְּחִלָּה עוֹבְדֵי עֲבוֹדָה זָרָה הָיוּ אֲבוֹתֵינוּ, וְעַכְשָׁיו קֵרְבָנוּ הַמָּקוֹם לַעֲבֹדָתוֹ, שֶׁנֶּאֱמַר: וַיֹּאמֶר יְהוֹשֻׁעַ אֶל כָּל הָעָם, כֹּה אָמַר יְיָ אֱלֹהֵי יִשְׂרָאֵל: בְּעֵבֶר הַנָּהָר יָשְׁבוּ אֲבוֹתֵיכֶם מֵעוֹלָם, תֶּרַח אֲבִי אַבְרָהָם וַאֲבִי נָחוֹר, וַיַּעַבְדוּ אֱלֹהִים אֲחֵרִים. וָאֶקַּח אֶת אֲבִיכֶם אֶת אַבְרָהָם מֵעֵבֶר הַנָּהָר וָאוֹלֵךְ אוֹתוֹ בְּכָל אֶרֶץ כְּנָעַן, וָאַרְבֶּה אֶת זַרְעוֹ וָאֶתֵּן לוֹ אֶת יִצְחָק, וָאֶתֵּן לְיִצְחָק אֶת יַעֲקֹב וְאֶת עֵשָׂו. וָאֶתֵּן לְעֵשָׂו אֶת הַר שֵׂעִיר לָרֶשֶׁת אֹתוֹ, וְיַעֲקֹב וּבָנָיו יָרְדוּ מִצְרָיִם.

Mi-techilah ovdey avodah zarah hayu avoteynu, v'achshav kervanu ha-makom la'avodato, she-ne'emar: va-yomer Yehoshua el kol ha-am, koh amar Adonay Elohey Yisrael: b'ever ha-nahar yashvu avoteychem me'olam, terach avi Avraham v'avi nachor, va-ya'avdu Elohim acherim. Va-ekach et avichem v'et Avraham me-ever ha-nahar va-olech oto b'chol eretz kena'an, va-arbeh et zar'o va-eten lo et Yitzhak, va-eten l'yitzhak et Ya'akov v'et Esav. Va-eten l'esav et har se'ir lareshet oto, v'ya'akov u'vanav yardu mitsrayma.

In the beginning, our forefathers served idols but now G-d has brought us close to His service, as it is said: and Joshua said to all the people: Thus said the L rd, the G d of Israel: Once, your fathers lived on the other side of the river – Terach, father of Abraham and Nahor, and they worshipped other gods. Then, I led your father Abraham across the river and all over the land of Canaan, and gave him many sons, including Yitzhak, and to Yitzhak I gave Jacob and Esaw. To Esaw I gave Mount Se'ir, and Jacob and his sons traveled to Egypt.

Magid

בָּרוּךְ שׁוֹמֵר הַבְטָחָתוֹ לְיִשְׂרָאֵל, בָּרוּךְ הוּא. שֶׁהַקָּדוֹשׁ בָּרוּךְ הוּא חִשַּׁב אֶת הַקֵּץ, לַעֲשׂוֹת כְּמָה שֶׁאָמַר לְאַבְרָהָם אָבִינוּ בִּבְרִית בֵּין הַבְּתָרִים, שֶׁנֶּאֱמַר: וַיֹּאמֶר לְאַבְרָם, יָדֹעַ תֵּדַע כִּי גֵר יִהְיֶה זַרְעֲךָ בְּאֶרֶץ לֹא לָהֶם, וַעֲבָדוּם וְעִנּוּ אֹתָם אַרְבַּע מֵאוֹת שָׁנָה. וְגַם אֶת הַגּוֹי אֲשֶׁר יַעֲבֹדוּ דָּן אָנֹכִי וְאַחֲרֵי כֵן יֵצְאוּ בִּרְכֻשׁ גָּדוֹל.

Baruch shomer havtachato l'Yisrael, baruch hu. She-ha-kadosh Baruch Hu chishav et ha-ketz, la'asot kemo she-am-ar l'Avraham avinu bi-vrit beyn ha-betarim, she-ne'emar: va-yomer l'Avraham, yado'a teda ki ger yihiyeh zar'acha b'eretz lo lahem, va-avadum v'inu otam arba me'ot shanah. V'gam et ha-goy ashery a-avdu dan anochi v'acharey chen yet-su bi-rechush gadol.

Blessed is He who keeps his promise to Israel, blessed is He. For He who is holy expected the end, and did as He had said to our father Abraham at the in their covenant, as it is said: and He said to Abraham, you shall know that your seed will be strangers in a foreign land, and they will be enslaved and made to suffer for four hundred years. But I shall judge the nation whom they shall serve, and after that they will come out with great wealth.'"

☞ *Raise your full cup of wine and say together:*

וְהִיא שֶׁעָמְדָה לַאֲבוֹתֵינוּ וְלָנוּ. שֶׁלֹא אֶחָד בִּלְבָד עָמַד עָלֵינוּ לְכַלּוֹתֵנוּ, אֶלָּא שֶׁבְּכָל דּוֹר וָדוֹר עוֹמְדִים עָלֵינוּ לְכַלּוֹתֵנוּ, וְהַקָּדוֹשׁ בָּרוּךְ הוּא מַצִּילֵנוּ מִיָּדָם.

V'hi she-amda l'avoteynu v'lanu.
She-lo echad bilvad amad aleynu l'chaloteinu, ela she-b'chol dor v'dor, omdim aleynu l'chaloteinu, v'ha-Kadosh Baruch Hu matsileynu m'yadam.

This promise has been upheld for our ancestors and for us.

For over the years, every generation, there have been those who have wanted to defeat and annihilate us, and G-d, Blessed be His Name, has saved us from them time and time again.

The Jewish people have endured for many, many centuries, despite abundant persecution and hate.

This is mainly thanks to our strong connection to our heritage and the lengths Jewish communities, both orthodox and reform, go to in order to preserve our rich history.

Sitting down with our loved ones to celebrate Passover year after year in the way it was meant to be celebrated is one way we modern Jews can ensure that our tradition lives on and stays strong, even in the face of adversity.

 Put down the cup of wine.

The Ten Plagues

אֵלּוּ עֶשֶׂר מַכּוֹת שֶׁהֵבִיא הַקָּדוֹשׁ בָּרוּךְ הוּא עַל הַמִּצְרִים בְּמִצְרַיִם, וְאֵלּוּ הֵן:

Eylu eser ha-makot she-hevi ha-Kadosh Baruch Hu al ha-mitsrim b'mitsrayim, v'eylu hen:

These are the ten plagues that G-d, Blessed be His Name, brought down upon the Egyptians in Egypt:

 As you recite the ten plagues, pour a drop of wine from your cup onto a plate for each.

דָּם Dam **Blood**

צְפַרְדֵּעַ Tsfardeya **Frogs**

כִּנִּים Kinim **Lice**

עָרוֹב Arov **Wild Beasts**

Magid

דֶּבֶר Dever **Plague**

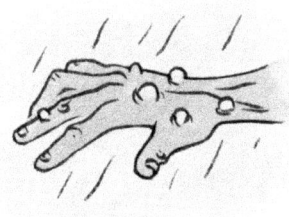

שְׁחִין Shechin **Boils**

בָּרָד Barad **Hail**

אַרְבֶּה Arbeh **Locusts**

חֹשֶׁךְ Choshech **Darkness**

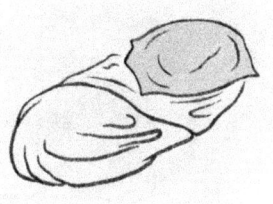

מַכַּת בְּכוֹרוֹת Makat Bechorot
Slaying of the Firstborn

רַבִּי יְהוּדָה הָיָה נוֹתֵן בָּהֶם סִמָּנִים: Rabi Yehudah hayah noten ba-hem simanim:

Rabbi Yehuda would assign them mnemonics:

דְּצַ"ךְ	Detsach (blood, frogs, lice)
עֲדַ"שׁ	Adash (wild beasts, plague, boils)
בְּאַחַ"ב	B'achav (hail, locusts, darkness, slaying of the firstborn)

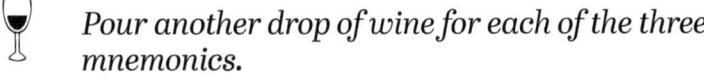 *Pour another drop of wine for each of the three mnemonics.*

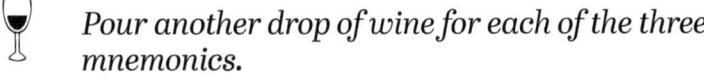 *Remove the cup of wine and the plate with the wine you spilled and refill your second cup of wine.*

The Egyptians were plagued by misfortunes brought down upon on them by a divine hand.

Today, we are plagued by man-made injustices. Take a moment to think about those of us who still suffer under the weight of modern-day plagues and how we can overcome them:

1. **Inequality** – be it due to race, gender, religion, sexual orientation, social status, creed, or skin color, not everyone in our world enjoys equal opportunities.

2. **Stigma** – although our world is more progressive in the 21st century than it has ever been before, we still have a long way to go. Stigmas surrounding mental health, weight, substance use, gender identity, and many more endure to this day and are best left behind in the past.

3. **Homelessness** – being without a safe, warm home to come back to is unimaginable to most but a reality for many.

4. **Hunger** – as we feast on the many delicacies of the Seder table, we should remember our fellow humans who are not as lucky as we are and cannot always put a full, hearty meal on the table.

5. **Domestic violence** – people suffering from domestic abuse are often unseen and their voice unheard. Being fearful in your own home is something no man, woman, or child should ever have to endure.

6. **Greed** – with the resources available to us today, greed has become a plague to humanity. We want more – more money, more recognition, more followers, more luxury – and sometimes, we lose sight of what truly matters.

7. **Climate destruction** – we have only one world to live in, and it is our responsibility to look after it. We must appreciate the many gifts our planet bestows on us and care for it as we would our home.

8. **Affordable education** – everyone deserves the chance for a well-rounded, effective education. Unfortunately, even in Western culture, some members of the community are denied this basic right, keeping them on the sidelines of society.

9. **Distraction** – in an age of screens and quick entertainment, it is easy to lose sight of what is important. When we contend with such huge barrages of information every minute of the day, it is hard to give time to important things like personal connection and quiet introspection.

10. **Gun violence** – unfortunately a unique plague to the US, Americans find themselves living a reality today where gun violence is so widespread that it has become a real and constant threat to many children and adults.

Magid

רַבִּי יוֹסֵי הַגְּלִילִי אוֹמֵר: מִנַּיִן אַתָּה אוֹמֵר שֶׁלָּקוּ הַמִּצְרִים בְּמִצְרַיִם עֶשֶׂר מַכּוֹת וְעַל הַיָּם לָקוּ חֲמִשִּׁים מַכּוֹת?

בְּמִצְרַיִם מָה הוּא אוֹמֵר? וַיֹּאמְרוּ הַחַרְטֻמִּים אֶל פַּרְעֹה: אֶצְבַּע אֱלֹהִים הִיא, וְעַל הַיָּם מָה הוּא אוֹמֵר? וַיַּרְא יִשְׂרָאֵל אֶת הַיָּד הַגְּדֹלָה אֲשֶׁר עָשָׂה יְיָ בְּמִצְרַיִם, וַיִּירְאוּ הָעָם אֶת יְיָ, וַיַּאֲמִינוּ בַּיְיָ וּבְמֹשֶׁה עַבְדּוֹ. כַּמָּה לָקוּ בְאֶצְבַּע? עֶשֶׂר מַכּוֹת. אֱמוֹר מֵעַתָּה: בְּמִצְרַיִם לָקוּ עֶשֶׂר מַכּוֹת וְעַל הַיָּם לָקוּ חֲמִשִּׁים מַכּוֹת.

Rabi Yosey ha-glili omer: mi-nayin atah omer she-laku ha-mitzrim b'mitzrayim eser makot v'al ha-yam laku chamishim makot?

B'mitzrayim ma hu omer? Va-yomru ha-chartumim el paroh: etsba Elohim hi, v'al ha-yam me hu omer? Va-yar Yisrael et ha-yad ha-gedolah asher asa Adonay b'mitsrayim, va-yiru ha-am et Adonay, va-ya'aminu b'Adonay u'v'moshe avdo. Kama laku v'etsba? Eser makot. Emor me'ata: b'mits-rayim laku eser makot v'al ha-yam laku chamishim makot.

Rabbi Yossey of the Galillei would ask: how do we know that the Egyptians were struck by ten plagues in Egypt and fifty plagues at sea?

In Egypt, what does it say? And the magicians said to Pharaoh: it is the hand of G-d. And at sea, what does it say? And Israel saw the mighty hand that G-d swept upon Egypt, and they feared G-d and trusted in Him and in Moses, his servant. Hoy many were they struck by the hand? Ten plagues. Thus, you shall say from now on: In Egypt they were struck by ten plagues and at sea they were struck by fifty plagues.

רַבִּי אֱלִיעֶזֶר אוֹמֵר: מִנַּיִן שֶׁכָּל מַכָּה וּמַכָּה שֶׁהֵבִיא הַקָּדוֹשׁ בָּרוּךְ הוּא עַל הַמִּצְרִים בְּמִצְרַיִם הָיְתָה שֶׁל אַרְבַּע מַכּוֹת?

שֶׁנֶּאֱמַר: יְשַׁלַּח בָּם חֲרוֹן אַפּוֹ, עֶבְרָה וָזַעַם וְצָרָה, מִשְׁלַחַת מַלְאֲכֵי רָעִים. עֶבְרָה – אַחַת, וָזַעַם – שְׁתַּיִם, וְצָרָה – שָׁלֹש, מִשְׁלַחַת מַלְאֲכֵי רָעִים – אַרְבַּע. אֱמוֹר מֵעַתָּה: בְּמִצְרַיִם לָקוּ אַרְבָּעִים מַכּוֹת וְעַל הַיָּם לָקוּ מָאתַיִם מַכּוֹת.

Rabi Eliezer omer: mi-nayin she-kol makah v'makah she-hevi ha-Kadosh Baruch Hu al ha-mitsrim b'mitsrayim haytah shel arba makot?

She-ne'emar: yishlach bahem charon apo, evrah v'za'am v'tsarah, mishlachat mal'achei ra'im. Evra – achat, v'za'am – shtayim, v'tsarah – shalosh, mishlachat mal'achei ra'im – arba. Emor me-atah: b'mitsrayim laku arba'im makot v'al ha-yam laku matayim makot.

Rabbi Eliezer would ask: how do we know that each plague inflicted by G-d on the Egyptians in Egypt was worth four plagues?

It is said: and he unleashed upon them his rage, anger and wrath and troubles, a delegation of messengers of evil. Anger – is one, wrath – makes two, troubles – make three, and messengers of evil make four. Thus, you shall say from now on: In Egypt they were struck by forty plagues, and at sea they were struck by two hundred plagues.

Magid

רַבִּי עֲקִיבָא אוֹמֵר: מִנַּיִן שֶׁכָּל מַכָּה וּמַכָּה שֶׁהֵבִיא הַקָּדוֹשׁ בָּרוּךְ הוּא עַל הַמִּצְרִים בְּמִצְרַיִם הָיְתָה שֶׁל חָמֵשׁ מַכּוֹת?

שֶׁנֶּאֱמַר: יְשַׁלַּח בָּם חֲרוֹן אַפּוֹ, עֶבְרָה וָזַעַם וְצָרָה, מִשְׁלַחַת מַלְאֲכֵי רָעִים. חֲרוֹן אַפּוֹ - אַחַת, עֶבְרָה - שְׁתַּיִם, וָזַעַם - שָׁלֹשׁ, וְצָרָה - אַרְבַּע, מִשְׁלַחַת מַלְאֲכֵי רָעִים - חָמֵשׁ. אֱמוֹר מֵעַתָּה: בְּמִצְרַיִם לָקוּ חֲמִשִּׁים מַכּוֹת וְעַל הַיָּם לָקוּ חֲמִשִּׁים וּמָאתַיִם מַכּוֹת.

Rabi Akiva omer: mi-nayin she-kol makah v'makah she-hevi ha-Kadosh Baruch Hu al ha-mitsrim b'mitsrayim hayta shel chamesh makot?

She-ne'emar: yishlach bam charon apo, evrah v'za'am v'tsarah, mishlachat mal'achei ra'im. Charon apo – achat, evra – shtayim, v'za'am – shalosh, v'tsarah – arba, mishlachat mal'achei ra'im – chamesh. Emor me-atah: b'mitsrayim laku chamishim makot v'al ha-yam laku chamishim u'matay-im makot.

Rabbi Akiva would ask: how do we know that each plague inflicted by G-d on the Egyptians in Egypt was worth five plagues?

It is said: and he unleashed upon them his rage, anger and wrath and troubles, a delegation of messengers of evil. Rage – is one, anger – makes two, wrath – makes three, troubles – make four, and messengers of evil make five. Thus, you shall say from now on: In Egypt they were struck by fifty plagues, and at sea they were struck by fifty and two hundred plagues.

Dayeinu

כַּמָּה מַעֲלוֹת טוֹבוֹת לַמָּקוֹם עָלֵינוּ!

Kama ma'alot tovot la-makom aleynu!

אִלּוּ הוֹצִיאָנוּ מִמִּצְרַיִם וְלֹא עָשָׂה בָהֶם שְׁפָטִים, דַּיֵּינוּ.

Ilu hotsi'anu m'mitsrayim v'lo asah vahem shefatim, dayeinu.

אִלּוּ עָשָׂה בָהֶם שְׁפָטִים, וְלֹא עָשָׂה בֵאלֹהֵיהֶם, דַּיֵּינוּ.

Ilu asah behm shefatim v'lo asah b'eloheyhem, dayeinu.

אִלּוּ עָשָׂה בֵאלֹהֵיהֶם, וְלֹא הָרַג אֶת בְּכוֹרֵיהֶם, דַּיֵּינוּ.

Ilu asah b'eloheyhem v'lo harag et bechoreyhem, dayeinu.

אִלּוּ הָרַג אֶת בְּכוֹרֵיהֶם וְלֹא נָתַן לָנוּ אֶת מָמוֹנָם, דַּיֵּינוּ.

Ilu harag et bechoreyhem v'lo natan lanu et mamonam, dayeinu.

אִלּוּ נָתַן לָנוּ אֶת מָמוֹנָם וְלֹא קָרַע לָנוּ אֶת הַיָּם, דַּיֵּינוּ.

Ilu natan lanu et mamonam v'lo kara lanu et hayam, dayeinu.

אִלּוּ קָרַע לָנוּ אֶת הַיָּם וְלֹא הֶעֱבִירָנוּ בְתוֹכוֹ בֶּחָרָבָה, דַּיֵּינוּ.

Ilu kara lanu et hayam v'lo he'eyviranu betocho b'charavah, dayeinu.

אִלּוּ הֶעֱבִירָנוּ בְתוֹכוֹ בֶּחָרָבָה וְלֹא שִׁקַּע צָרֵנוּ בְּתוֹכוֹ, דַּיֵּינוּ.

Ilu he'eyviranu betocho b'charavah v'lo shika tsareynu betocho, dayeinu.

אִלּוּ שִׁקַּע צָרֵנוּ בְּתוֹכוֹ וְלֹא סִפֵּק צָרְכֵּנוּ בַּמִּדְבָּר אַרְבָּעִים שָׁנָה, דַּיֵּינוּ.

Ilu shika tsareynu betocho v'lo sipek tsarcheynu ba-midbar arba'im shanah, dayeinu.

אִלּוּ סִפֵּק צָרְכֵּנוּ בַּמִּדְבָּר אַרְבָּעִים שָׁנָה וְלֹא הֶאֱכִילָנוּ אֶת הַמָּן, דַּיֵּינוּ.

Ilu sipek tsarcheynu ba-midbar arba'im shanah v'lo he'eychilanu et ha-man, dayeinu.

Magid

אִלּוּ הֶאֱכִילָנוּ אֶת הַמָּן וְלֹא נָתַן לָנוּ אֶת הַשַּׁבָּת, דַּיֵּינוּ.	Ilu he'eychilanu et ha-man v'lo natan lanu et ha-shabbat, dayeinu.
אִלּוּ קֵרְבָנוּ לִפְנֵי הַר סִינַי, וְלֹא נָתַן לָנוּ אֶת הַתּוֹרָה, דַּיֵּינוּ.	Ilu natan lanu et ha-shabbat v'lo kervanu lifney har sinai, dayeinu.
אִלּוּ נָתַן לָנוּ אֶת הַשַּׁבָּת, וְלֹא קֵרְבָנוּ לִפְנֵי הַר סִינַי, דַּיֵּינוּ.	Ilu kervanu lifney har sinai v'lo natan lanu et ha-torah, dayeinu.
אִלּוּ נָתַן לָנוּ אֶת הַתּוֹרָה וְלֹא הִכְנִיסָנוּ לְאֶרֶץ יִשְׂרָאֵל, דַּיֵּינוּ.	Ilu natan lanu et ha-torah v'lo hichnisanu l'eretz yisrael, dayeinu.
אִלּוּ הִכְנִיסָנוּ לְאֶרֶץ יִשְׂרָאֵל וְלֹא בָּנָה לָנוּ אֶת בֵּית הַבְּחִירָה, דַּיֵּינוּ.	Ilu hichnisanu l'eretz Yisrael v'lo vana lanu et beyt ha-behira, dayeinu.

How many good favors G-d has bestowed upon us!

Had He liberated us from Egypt and not carried out justice against the Egyptians, we would have been grateful enough.

Had He carried out justice against the Egyptians and not against their gods, we would have been grateful enough.

Had He carried out justice against their gods and not slain their firstborns, we would have been grateful enough.

Had He slain their firstborns and not given us their treasures, we would have been grateful enough.

Had He given us their treasures and not split the sea for us, we would have been grateful enough.

Had He split the sea for us and not let us through it on dry land, we would have been grateful enough.

Had He led us through the sea on dry land and not drowned our enemies in it, we would have been grateful enough.

Had He drowned our enemies in the sea and not provided for us in the desert for forty years, we would have been grateful enough.

Had He provided for us in the desert for forty years and not given us the manna, we would have been grateful enough.

Had He given us the manna and not given us the Sabbath, we would have been grateful enough.

Had He given us the Sabbath and not brought us to Mount Sinai, we would have been grateful enough.

Had He brought us to Mount Sinai and not given us the Torah, we would have been grateful enough.

Had He given us the Torah and not brought us into Israel, we would have been grateful enough.

Had He brought us into Israel and not built the Temple of worship, we would have been grateful enough.

Magid

Meaning "enough", Dayeinu once again highlights the Jewish value of gratitude.

It is no simple thing to be satisfied with what you have, particularly in an era when plenty and abundance are so easily available. We tend to always want more – more clothes, more money, more friends, more luxuries. But Dayeinu says to us, stop. Think about all the things you already have. Aren't they enough?

Just as we can be thankful for all the myriad miracles bestowed upon us as we left enslavement in Egypt, so should we be able today, in a time of such plenty, to give thanks for the gifts we have been granted in life.

The Symbols of Passover

רַבָּן גַּמְלִיאֵל הָיָה אוֹמֵר: כָּל שֶׁלֹּא אָמַר שְׁלשָׁה דְּבָרִים אֵלּוּ בַּפֶּסַח, לֹא יָצָא יְדֵי חוֹבָתוֹ, וְאֵלּוּ הֵן:

Raban Gamilel hayah womer: kol she-lo amar ahloshah devarim eylu ba-pesach, lo yatsa yedey chovato, v'eylu hen:

Rabbi Gamliel would say, all who have not recited these three things on Passover have not done their duty. And these things are:

All say together:

פֶּסַח, מַצָּה, וּמָרוֹר.   Pesach, matzah, u'maror.

Pesach, Matzah, and Bitter Herbs.

Magid

פֶּסַח שֶׁהָיוּ אֲבוֹתֵינוּ אוֹכְלִים בִּזְמַן שֶׁבֵּית הַמִּקְדָּשׁ הָיָה קַיָּם, עַל שׁוּם מָה?

עַל שׁוּם שֶׁפָּסַח הַקָּדוֹשׁ בָּרוּךְ הוּא עַל בָּתֵּי אֲבוֹתֵינוּ בְּמִצְרַיִם, שֶׁנֶּאֱמַר: וַאֲמַרְתֶּם זֶבַח פֶּסַח הוּא לַיָי, אֲשֶׁר פָּסַח עַל בָּתֵּי בְנֵי יִשְׂרָאֵל בְּמִצְרַיִם בְּנָגְפּוֹ אֶת מִצְרַיִם, וְאֶת בָּתֵּינוּ הִצִּיל, וַיִּקֹּד הָעָם וַיִּשְׁתַּחֲווּ.

Pesach she-hayu avoteynu ochlim bizman she-beyt ha-mikdash hayah kayam, al shum mah?
Al shum she-pasach ha-Kadosh Baruch Hu al batey avoteynu b'mitsrayim, she-ne'emar: v'amartem zevach pesach hu l'Adonai, asher pasach al batey bney Yisrael b'mitsrayim b'nogfo et mitsrayim, v'et bateynu hitsil, vayikod ha'am vayishtachavu.

Pesach, the sacrificial offering that our ancestors would eat while the Temple was standing. What is the meaning of it?

In memory of how G-d passed over the homes of our ancestors in Egypt, sparing them. As it is said: The Pesach is an offering to G-d, who passed over the homes of the Israelites in Egypt as He smote the Egyptians and saved our homes. And the people bowed and genuflected before Him.

☞ *Raise the matzah and say:*

מַצָּה זוֹ שֶׁאָנוּ אוֹכְלִים, עַל שׁוּם מָה? עַל שׁוּם שֶׁלֹּא הִסְפִּיק בְּצֵקָם שֶׁל אֲבוֹתֵינוּ לְהַחֲמִיץ עַד שֶׁנִּגְלָה עֲלֵיהֶם מֶלֶךְ מַלְכֵי הַמְּלָכִים, הַקָּדוֹשׁ בָּרוּךְ הוּא, וּגְאָלָם, שֶׁנֶּאֱמַר: וַיֹּאפוּ אֶת הַבָּצֵק אֲשֶׁר הוֹצִיאוּ מִמִּצְרַיִם עֻגֹת מַצּוֹת, כִּי לֹא חָמֵץ, כִּי גֹרְשׁוּ מִמִּצְרַיִם וְלֹא יָכְלוּ לְהִתְמַהְמֵהַּ, וְגַם צֵדָה לֹא עָשׂוּ לָהֶם.

Matzah zo she-anu ochlim. Al shum mah?

Al shum she-lo hispik betsekam ahel avoteynu l'hachmitz ad she-niglah aleyhem Melech malchei ha-mlachim, Ha-Kadosh Baruch Hu, u'gealam, she-ne'emar: vayofu et ha-batsek asher hotsi'u m'mitsrayim ugot matzot, ki lo chametz, ki gorshu m'mitsrayim v'lo yachlu l'hit-mahamehah, v'gam tseydah lo asu lahem.

Matzah, this unleavened bread that we eat, what is the meaning of it?

In memory of the unleavened bread that our ancestors made and did not have time to rise before the King of Kings, G-d, Blessed be His Name, appeared before them and redeemed them. It is said: and they baked the dough that they brought with them from Egypt into matzahs, because it did not rise, as they were banished from Egypt and could not delay and did not even have time to prepare provisions.

Magid

👉 *Raise the maror and say:*

מָרוֹר זֶה שֶׁאָנוּ אוֹכְלִים, עַל שׁוּם מָה?
עַל שׁוּם שֶׁמֵּרְרוּ הַמִּצְרִים אֶת חַיֵּי אֲבוֹתֵינוּ בְּמִצְרַיִם, שֶׁנֶּאֱמַר: וַיְמָרֲרוּ אֶת חַיֵּיהֶם בַּעֲבֹדָה קָשָׁה, בְּחֹמֶר וּבִלְבֵנִים וּבְכָל עֲבֹדָה בַּשָּׂדֶה אֵת כָּל עֲבֹדָתָם אֲשֶׁר עָבְדוּ בָהֶם בְּפָרֶךְ.

Maror ze she-anu ochlim, al shum mah?
Al shum she-mereyru hamitsrim et chayey avoteinu b'mitsrayim, she-ne'emar: vayemareru et chayeyhem b'avoda kasha, b'chomer u'vilvenim u'vechol avoda ba-sadeh et kol avodatam asher avdu baheym b'farech

Maror, these bitter herbs that we eat, what is the meaning of it?

In memory of the bitterness that the Egyptians inflicted on the lives of our ancestors. It is said: and they made their lives bitter with hard labor, with mortar and bricks, work in the fields and every form of slavery that they forced upon them.

בְּכָל דּוֹר וָדוֹר חַיָּב אָדָם לִרְאוֹת אֶת עַצְמוֹ כְּאִלּוּ הוּא יָצָא מִמִּצְרַיִם, שֶׁנֶּאֱמַר: וְהִגַּדְתָּ לְבִנְךָ בַּיּוֹם הַהוּא לֵאמֹר, בַּעֲבוּר זֶה עָשָׂה יְיָ לִי בְּצֵאתִי מִמִּצְרָיִם.

B'chol dor va'dor chayav adam lirot et atsmo ke'ilu hu yatsa m'mitsrayim, she-ne'emar: v'higadta l'vincha bayom hahu l'emor: ba'avur ze asah Adonai li b'tseyti m'mitsrayim.

In every generation, every person must see themselves as though they had been liberated from Egypt, as it is said: and on that day, you shall tell your child all that G-d did for you when He set you free from Egypt.

לֹא אֶת אֲבוֹתֵינוּ בִּלְבַד גָּאַל הַקָּדוֹשׁ בָּרוּךְ הוּא, אֶלָּא אַף אוֹתָנוּ גָּאַל עִמָּהֶם, שֶׁנֶּאֱמַר: וְאוֹתָנוּ הוֹצִיא מִשָּׁם, לְמַעַן הָבִיא אוֹתָנוּ, לָתֶת לָנוּ אֶת הָאָרֶץ אֲשֶׁר נִשְׁבַּע לַאֲבֹתֵינוּ.

Lo et avoteynu bilvad ga'al ha-Kadosh Baruch Hu, ela af otanu ga'al imahem, she-ne'emar: v'otanu hotsi mi'sham, l'ma'an hevi otanu, latet lanu et ha-aretz asher nishba l'avoteynu.

Not only our forefathers did G-d, blessed be His name, redeem, but He redeemed us alongside them, as it is said: and He removed us from there, to deliver us, to give us the land that he swore to our ancestors

לְפִיכָךְ אֲנַחְנוּ חַיָּבִים לְהוֹדוֹת, לְהַלֵּל, לְשַׁבֵּחַ, לְפָאֵר, לְרוֹמֵם, לְהַדֵּר, לְבָרֵךְ, לְעַלֵּה וּלְקַלֵּס לְמִי שֶׁעָשָׂה לַאֲבוֹתֵינוּ וְלָנוּ אֶת כָּל הַנִּסִּים הָאֵלּוּ: הוֹצִיאָנוּ מֵעַבְדוּת לְחֵרוּת מִיָּגוֹן לְשִׂמְחָה, וּמֵאֵבֶל לְיוֹם טוֹב, וּמֵאֲפֵלָה לְאוֹר גָּדוֹל, וּמִשִּׁעְבּוּד לִגְאֻלָּה. וְנֹאמַר לְפָנָיו: הַלְלוּיָהּ.

L'fichach anachnu chayavim l'hodot, l'halel, l'shabeyach, l'fa'er, l'romem, l'hader, l'vareych, l'aleh u'l'kaleys l'mi she-asa l'avoteynu v'lanu et kol ha-nisim ha'eylu: hotsi'anu m'avdut l'cheyrut m'yagon l'simcha, u'm'eyvel l'yom tov, u'm'afeyla l'or gadol, u'm'shi'abud li-g'ula. V'nomar lefanav, halleluyah.

Therefore, we must give thanks, praise, glorify, exalt, laud, revere, bless, magnify, and extol He who did for our forefathers and for us all of these miracles: delivered us from slavery to freedom, from sorrow to joy, from grief to celebration, from darkness to light, and from subjugation to redemption. And to Him we say, hallelujah.

Magid

הַלְלוּ יָהּ הַלְלוּ עַבְדֵי יְהוָה הַלְלוּ אֶת שֵׁם יְהוָה. יְהִי שֵׁם יְהוָה מְבֹרָךְ מֵעַתָּה וְעַד עוֹלָם. מִמִּזְרַח שֶׁמֶשׁ עַד מְבוֹאוֹ מְהֻלָּל שֵׁם יְהוָה. רָם עַל כָּל גּוֹיִם יְהוָה עַל הַשָּׁמַיִם כְּבוֹדוֹ. מִי כַּיהוָה אֱלֹהֵינוּ הַמַּגְבִּיהִי לָשָׁבֶת. הַמַּשְׁפִּילִי לִרְאוֹת בַּשָּׁמַיִם וּבָאָרֶץ. מְקִימִי מֵעָפָר דָּל מֵאַשְׁפֹּת יָרִים אֶבְיוֹן. לְהוֹשִׁיבִי עִם נְדִיבִים עִם נְדִיבֵי עַמּוֹ. מוֹשִׁיבִי עֲקֶרֶת הַבַּיִת אֵם הַבָּנִים שְׂמֵחָה הַלְלוּיָהּ.

Halleluya heleylu avdey Adonay haleylu et shem Adonai. Yehi shem Adonai mevorach m'ata v'ad olam. Mi-mizrach shemesh ad mevo'o mehulal shem Adonay. Ram al kol goyim Adonay al ha-shamayim kevodo. Mi k'Adonay eloheynu ha'magbihi lashavet. Ha-mashpili lirot ba-shamayim u'va-aretz. Mekimi m'afar dal m'ashpot yarim evyon. L'hoshivi im nedivim im nedivey amo. Moshivi akeret ha-bayit em ha-banim semeycha halleluyah.

Praise the Lord, servants of G-d, praise G-d's name. May G-d's name be blessed from now and forever. From the sun in the East until its approach G-d's name is exalted. G-d is greater than any nation and His honor dwells in the sky. Who is like the Lord our G-d, who resides in the heavens. Who deigns to look down upon heavens and earth. He raises the poor from the dust and the needy from the ashes. He puts me with the most generous of His people. He brings joy to the housewife, mother of children. Halleluyah.

בְּצֵאת יִשְׂרָאֵל מִמִּצְרָיִם בֵּית יַעֲקֹב מֵעַם לֹעֵז. הָיְתָה יְהוּדָה לְקָדְשׁוֹ יִשְׂרָאֵל מַמְשְׁלוֹתָיו. הַיָּם רָאָה וַיָּנֹס הַיַּרְדֵּן יִסֹּב לְאָחוֹר. הֶהָרִים רָקְדוּ כְאֵילִים גְּבָעוֹת כִּבְנֵי צֹאן. מַה לְּךָ הַיָּם כִּי תָנוּס הַיַּרְדֵּן תִּסֹּב לְאָחוֹר. הֶהָרִים תִּרְקְדוּ כְאֵילִים גְּבָעוֹת כִּבְנֵי צֹאן. מִלִּפְנֵי אָדוֹן חוּלִי אָרֶץ מִלִּפְנֵי אֱלוֹהַּ יַעֲקֹב. הַהֹפְכִי הַצּוּר אֲגַם מָיִם חַלָּמִישׁ לְמַעְיְנוֹ מָיִם.

B'tseyt Yisrael m'mitzrayim beyt ya'akov me'am lo'ez. Hayta Yehuda l'kodsho Yisrael mamshelotav. Ha-yam ra'ah va-yanos ha-yarden yisov l'achor. He-harim rakdu k'eylim geva'ot kivney tson. Ma lecha ha-yam ki tanus ha-yarden tisov l'achor. He-harim tirkedu k'eylim geva'oy kivney tson. Mi-lifney Adonai chuli aretz mi-lifney eloha ya'akov. Ha-hofchi hatsur agam mayim chalamish l-mayno mayim.

When the Israelites left Egypt, when the house of Jacob left that foreign land, thus Jews hold Him sacred and Israel follow Him. The sea beheld and withdrew, the Jordan turned back. The mountains danced like rams, the hills like sheep and goats. Why do you withdraw, sea? Why do you turn back, Jordan? Mountains, dance like rams and hills, dance like sheep and goats. Before the Master of all, before the god of Jacob, the earth bows. You who can turn stone into water, flint into a spring.

Magid

בָּרוּךְ אַתָּה יְיָ אֱלֹהֵינוּ מֶלֶךְ הָעוֹלָם, אֲשֶׁר גְּאָלָנוּ וְגָאַל אֶת אֲבוֹתֵינוּ מִמִּצְרַיִם, וְהִגִּיעָנוּ לַלַּיְלָה הַזֶּה לֶאֱכָל בּוֹ מַצָּה וּמָרוֹר. כֵּן יְיָ אֱלֹהֵינוּ וֵאלֹהֵי אֲבוֹתֵינוּ יַגִּיעֵנוּ לְמוֹעֲדִים וְלִרְגָלִים אֲחֵרִים הַבָּאִים לִקְרָאתֵנוּ לְשָׁלוֹם, שְׂמֵחִים בְּבִנְיַן עִירֶךָ וְשָׂשִׂים בַּעֲבוֹדָתֶךָ. וְנֹאכַל שָׁם מִן הַזְּבָחִים וּמִן הַפְּסָחִים אֲשֶׁר יַגִּיעַ דָּמָם עַל קִיר מִזְבַּחֲךָ לְרָצוֹן, וְנוֹדֶה לְךָ שִׁיר חָדָשׁ עַל גְּאֻלָּתֵנוּ וְעַל פְּדוּת נַפְשֵׁנוּ. בָּרוּךְ אַתָּה יְיָ גָּאַל יִשְׂרָאֵל.

Baruch ata Adonay eloheynu Melech ha-olam, asher ge'alanu v'ga'al et avoteynu mi-mitsrayim, v'hegiyanu la'lalyla hazeh l'echol bo matzah u'maror. Ken Adonay eloheynu v'elohey avoteynu y'gi'eynu l'mo'adim u'l'regalim acherim ha-bai'im likrateynu l'shalom, semeychim b'vinyan irecha v'sasim b'avodatecha. V'nochal sham min ha-zevachim u'min ha-pesachim asher yagiya damam al kir mizbacheycha l'ratzon, v'nodeh lecha shir chadash al ge'ulateynu v'al pedut nafsheynu. Baruch atah Adonay ga'al Yisrael.

Blessed are You, Lord our G-d, King of the universe, who delivered us and our forefathers from Egypt, and brought us to this night, to eat matzah and maror. Lord our G-d, G-d of our ancestors, so You shall deliver us to many forthcoming events and celebrations, and we will be joyful in the resurrection of Your city and happy in doing Your work. And there, we shall eat from the sacrifices and the offerings whose blood shall touch the walls of the altar, and thank you with a new song for our salvation and the redemption of our souls. Blessed are You, G-d, deliverer of Israel.

בָּרוּךְ אַתָּה יְיָ אֱלֹהֵינוּ מֶלֶךְ הָעוֹלָם בּוֹרֵא פְּרִי הַגָּפֶן.

Baruch atah Adonai Eloheinu melech ha-olam, borei peri ha-gafen.

Blessed are You, Lord our G-d, King of the universe, creator of the fruit of the vine.

 Drink the second cup of wine, reclining to the left.

Rachtzah

רַחְצָה

Washing Hands
(this time, with a blessing)

Rachtzah רָחְצָה

☞ *Wash your hands again, pouring water from a cup onto each hand three times.*

📜 *This time, recite the blessing:*

בָּרוּךְ אַתָּה יְיָ אֱלֹהֵינוּ מֶלֶךְ הָעוֹלָם, אֲשֶׁר קִדְּשָׁנוּ בְּמִצְוֹתָיו וְצִוָּנוּ עַל נְטִילַת יָדָיִם.

Baruch atah Adonai Eloheinu melech ha-olam, asher kide-shanu b'mitzvotav v'tzivanu al netilat yadayim.

Blessed are You, Lord our G-d, King of the universe, who has sanctified us with His commandments and commanded us to wash our hands.

Motzi-Matzah

מוֹצִיא מַצָּה

Blessing on the Matzah

Motzi-Matzah מוֹצִיא מַצָּה

☞ *Pick up the three matzahs – the two whole ones with the broken half in between them – and raise them in the air.*

📜 *Recite the blessing:*

בָּרוּךְ אַתָּה יְיָ אֱלֹהֵינוּ מֶלֶךְ הָעוֹלָם הַמּוֹצִיא לֶחֶם מִן הָאָרֶץ.

Baruch atah Adonai Eloheinu melech ha-olam, ha-motzi lech-em min ha-aretz.

Blessed are You, Lord our G-d, King of the universe, who produces bread from the earth.

☞ *Now, remove the bottom matzah from the pile and return it to its place. Holding only the top and middle matzahs, recite the following blessing:*

בָּרוּךְ אַתָּה יְיָ אֱלֹהֵינוּ מֶלֶךְ הָעוֹלָם, אֲשֶׁר קִדְּשָׁנוּ בְּמִצְוֹתָיו וְצִוָּנוּ עַל אֲכִילַת מַצָּה.

Baruch atah Adonai Eloheinu melech ha-olam, asher kide-shanu b'mitzvotav v'tzivanu al achilat matzah.

Blessed are You, Lord our G-d, King of the universe, who has sanctified us with His commandments and commanded us to eat matzah.

☞ *Break off pieces of the top and middle matzahs and distribute them around the table. The matzah should be eaten while reclining to the left.*

Maror

מָרוֹר

Bitter Herb

Maror מָרוֹר

☞ *Take a piece of maror (horseradish, lettuce, or another bitter herb) and dip it in the charoset.*

📜 *Recite the blessing before eating:*

בָּרוּךְ אַתָּה יְיָ אֱלֹהֵינוּ מֶלֶךְ הָעוֹלָם, אֲשֶׁר קִדְּשָׁנוּ בְּמִצְוֹתָיו וְצִוָּנוּ עַל אֲכִילַת מָרוֹר.

Baruch atah Adonai Eloheinu melech ha-olam, asher kideshanu b'mitzvotav v'tzivanu al achilat maror.

Blessed are You, Lord our G-d, King of the universe, who has sanctified us with His commandments and commanded us to eat a bitter herb.

☞ *Do not lean while eating the Maror.*

Korech

כּוֹרֵךְ

Maror Wrapped
in Matzah

Korech כּוֹרֵךְ

☞ *Take two pieces of matzah, put some maror between them, and dip everything in the charoset. You may also spread the charoset on the matzah, add the maror and eat it like a sandwich.*

Recite before eating:

זֵכֶר לְמִקְדָּשׁ כְּהִלֵּל. כֵּן עָשָׂה הִלֵּל בִּזְמַן שֶׁבֵּית הַמִּקְדָּשׁ הָיָה קַיָּם: הָיָה כּוֹרֵךְ פֶּסַח מַצָּה וּמָרוֹר וְאוֹכֵל בְּיַחַד, לְקַיֵּם מַה שֶׁנֶּאֱמַר: עַל מַצּוֹת וּמְרֹרִים יֹאכְלֻהוּ.

Zecher l'mikdash k'hillel. Ken asah hillel bizman she-beyt ha-mikdash hayah kayam. Hayah korech pesach matzah umaror v'ochel beyachad, lekayem mah she-ne'emar: al matzot umerorim yocheluhu.

In memory of the custom of Hillel in the days of the Temple. So Hillel would do while there was a temple: he would wrap the matzah with the maror and eat them together, to observe what is commanded: You shall eat it (the Passover sacrifice) on matzah and maror.

☞ *Recline to the left and eat the maror sandwich.*

Shulchan-Orech

שֻׁלְחָן עוֹרֵךְ

The Festive Meal

Shulchan-Orech שֻׁלְחָן עוֹרֵךְ

☞ *Now is the time to sit back, relax, and enjoy a delicious festive meal.*

☞ *At this point, it is customary to eat the hard-boiled egg from the Seder plate, dipped in salt water.*

Tzafun

צָפוּן

The Afikoman

Tzafun צָפוּן

☞ Now that you've finished the meal, it's time to reveal the Afikoman.

☞ If you hid it earlier in the evening, now is the time for whoever found it during the Seder to reveal it.

☞ The Afikoman is the last thing we eat during the Seder night. Break off pieces of the Afikoman matzah and distribute them around the table. Eat the matzah while reclining to your left.

Barech

בָּרֵךְ

Blessing After the Meal

Barech בָּרֵךְ

 Pour the third cup of wine.

 Recite the blessing on the wine:

בָּרוּךְ אַתָּה יְיָ אֱלֹהֵינוּ מֶלֶךְ הָעוֹלָם בּוֹרֵא פְּרִי הַגָּפֶן.

Baruch atah Adonai Eloheinu melech ha-olam, borei peri ha-gafen.

Blessed are You, Lord our G-d, King of the universe, creator of the fruit of the vine.

 Drink the third cup of wine, while reclining to the left.

 Pour the fourth cup of wine.

 It is customary to pour an extra cup of wine for Elijah the Prophet, who is said to visit on Seder night. Open the front door to invite him in.

Recite the following:

שְׁפֹךְ חֲמָתְךָ אֶל הַגּוֹיִם אֲשֶׁר לֹא יְדָעוּךָ וְעַל מַמְלָכוֹת אֲשֶׁר בְּשִׁמְךָ לֹא קָרָאוּ. כִּי אָכַל אֶת יַעֲקֹב וְאֶת נָוֵהוּ הֵשַׁמּוּ. שְׁפֹךְ עֲלֵיהֶם זַעְמֶךָ וַחֲרוֹן אַפְּךָ יַשִּׂיגֵם. תִּרְדֹּף בְּאַף וְתַשְׁמִידֵם מִתַּחַת שְׁמֵי יְיָ.

Shefoch chamatcha el ha-goyim asher lo yeda'ucha v'al mamlachot asher b'shimcha lo kar'u. Ki achal et ya'akov v'et navehu heyshamu. Shefoch aleyhem za'amcha v'charon apcha yasigem. Tirdof b'af v'tashmidem mitachat shmey Adonai.

Unleash Your wrath upon the nations who do not acknowledge You and upon the kingdoms who do not call Your Name. For they have devoured Jacob and destroyed his land. Unleash Your fury upon them and let Your anger seize them. Pursue them with rage and destroy them beneath G-d's heavens.

📜 *Some sing Eliyahu Ha'navi, which can be found in the "Songs" section on page 88.*

☞ *You may now close the front door.*

Hallel הַלֵּל

הִנְנִי מוּכָן וּמְזֻמָּן לְקַיֵּם מִצְוַת כּוֹס רְבִיעִי שֶׁהוּא כְּנֶגֶד בְּשׂוֹרַת הַיְשׁוּעָה, שֶׁאָמַר הַקָּדוֹשׁ בָּרוּךְ הוּא לְיִשְׂרָאֵל "וְלָקַחְתִּי אֶתְכֶם לִי לְעָם וְהָיִיתִי לָכֶם לֵאלֹהִים".

Hineyni muchan u'mezuman l'kayem mitzvat kos revi'i she-hu k'negged besorat ha-yeshu'a, she-amar ha-Kadosh Baruch Hu l'Yisrael, "v'lakachti etchem li l'am v'hayiti lachem l'elohim."

I am ready and willing to observe the commandment of the fourth cup, which signifies the tidings of salvation, as G-d said to the people of Israel: "and I will take you in as my people and I shall be your god."

 Now, make a blessing on the fourth cup of wine:

בָּרוּךְ אַתָּה יְיָ אֱלֹהֵינוּ מֶלֶךְ הָעוֹלָם בּוֹרֵא פְּרִי הַגָּפֶן.

Baruch atah Adonai Eloheinu melech ha-olam, borei peri ha-gafen.

Blessed are You, Lord our G-d, King of the universe, creator of the fruit of the vine.

 Drink the fourth and final cup of wine while reclining to the left.

Recite the final blessing after drinking wine:

בָּרוּךְ אַתָּה יְיָ אֱלֹהֵינוּ מֶלֶךְ הָעוֹלָם, עַל הַגֶּפֶן וְעַל פְּרִי הַגֶּפֶן, עַל תְּנוּבַת הַשָּׂדֶה וְעַל אֶרֶץ חֶמְדָּה טוֹבָה וּרְחָבָה שֶׁרָצִיתָ וְהִנְחַלְתָּ לַאֲבוֹתֵינוּ לֶאֱכֹל מִפִּרְיָהּ וְלִשְׂבֹּעַ מִטּוּבָהּ.

Baruch atah Adonai Eloheinu melech ha-olam, al ha-gefen v'al peri ha-gefen, al tnuvat ha-sadeh v'al eretz chemda tova u'rechava she-ratsita v'hinchalta l'avoteynu le'echol m'pirya v'lisbo'a mituva.

Blessed are You, Lord our G-d, King of the universe, for the vines and the fruit of the vines, for the produce of the field, and for the good, beautiful and vast country which You chose to give to our ancestors so that we may eat from its fruit and be satiated by its goodness.

רַחֵם נָא יְיָ אֱלֹהֵינוּ עַל יִשְׂרָאֵל עַמֶּךָ וְעַל יְרוּשָׁלַיִם עִירֶךָ וְעַל צִיּוֹן מִשְׁכַּן כְּבוֹדֶךָ וְעַל מִזְבְּחֶךָ וְעַל הֵיכָלֶךָ וּבְנֵה יְרוּשָׁלַיִם עִיר הַקֹּדֶשׁ בִּמְהֵרָה בְיָמֵינוּ וְהַעֲלֵנוּ לְתוֹכָהּ וְשַׂמְּחֵנוּ בְּבִנְיָנָהּ וְנֹאכַל מִפִּרְיָהּ וְנִשְׂבַּע מִטּוּבָהּ וּנְבָרֶכְךָ עָלֶיהָ בִּקְדֻשָּׁה וּבְטָהֳרָה.

Rachem na Adonai Eloheinu al Yisrael amcha v'al yerushalayim irecha v'al tsion mishkan kevodecha v'al mizbachecha v'al heichalecha u'vney yerushalayim ir ha-kodesh bimhera b'yameynu v'ha'aleynu l'tochah v'samchenu b'vinyanah v'nochal m'pirya v'nisba mituva u'nevarechecha aleyha b'kdusha uv'tahara.

Please have mercy, Lord our G-d, on Israel Your people, on Jerusalem Your city, on Zion, Your place of rest, on Your altar and Your hall. Rebuild the holy city of Jerusalem in our time and let us ascend to it and be joyous in its grandeur. Then we shall eat from its fruit and be satiated by its goodness and bless You for it with sanctity and purity.

בְּשַׁבָּת: וּרְצֵה וְהַחֲלִיצֵנוּ בְּיוֹם הַשַּׁבָּת הַזֶּה(וְשַׂמְּחֵנוּ בְּיוֹם חַג הַמַּצּוֹת הַזֶּה, כִּי אַתָּה יְיָ טוֹב וּמֵטִיב לַכֹּל וְנוֹדֶה לְךָ עַל הָאָרֶץ וְעַל פְּרִי הַגָּפֶן.

(on Shabbat: u'retsey v'hachalit-seynu b'yom ha-shabbat hazeh) v'samcheynu b'yom chag ha-matzot hazeh, ki atah Adonai tov u'meytiv lakol v'nodeh lecha al ha'aretz v'al peri ha-gafen.

(On Shabbat: Give us strength on this Sabbath day and) let us be happy on this festival of Matzah, because You are good and benevolent to all and we will thank You for the land and for the fruit of the vine.

בָּרוּךְ אַתָּה יְיָ עַל הָאָרֶץ וְעַל פְּרִי הַגָּפֶן.

Baruch ata Adonai, al ha'aretz v'al peri ha-gafen.

Blessed are You, G-d, for the land and for the fruit of the vine.

Nirtzah

נִרְצָה

Conclusion of the Seder

Nirtzah נִרְצָה

☞ At the conclusion of the Seder, we celebrate having been able to come together for the festivities and look forward to a prosperous and happy year. Everyone sings together:

לְשָׁנָה הַבָּאָה בִּירוּשָׁלָיִם.   L'shana haba'ah b'Yerushalayim

Next year in Jerusalem!

Songs

Chad Gadya – One Little Goat

חַד גַּדְיָא, חַד גַּדְיָא, דְּזַבִּין אַבָּא בִּתְרֵי זוּזֵי, חַד גַּדְיָא, חַד גַּדְיָא.

Chad gadya, chad gadya, d'zabin aba b'trei zuzei, chad gadya, chad gadya.

וְאָתָא שׁוּנְרָא וְאָכְלָה לְגַדְיָא, דְּזַבִּין אַבָּא בִּתְרֵי זוּזֵי, חַד גַּדְיָא, חַד גַּדְיָא.

V'ata shunra v'achla l'gadya, d'zabin aba b'trei zuzei, chad gadya, chad gadya.

וְאָתָא כַלְבָּא וְנָשַׁךְ לְשׁוּנְרָא, דְּאָכְלָה לְגַדְיָא, דְּזַבִּין אַבָּא בִּתְרֵי זוּזֵי, חַד גַּדְיָא, חַד גַּדְיָא.

V'ata chalba v'nashach l'shunra, d'achla l'gadya, d'zabin aba b'trei zuzei, chad gadya, chad gadya.

וְאָתָא חוּטְרָא וְהִכָּה לְכַלְבָּא, דְּנָשַׁךְ לְשׁוּנְרָא, דְּאָכְלָה לְגַדְיָא, דְּזַבִּין אַבָּא בִּתְרֵי זוּזֵי, חַד גַּדְיָא, חַד גַּדְיָא.

V'ata chutra v'hica l'calba, d'nashach l'shunra, d'achla l'gadya, d'zabin aba b'trei zuzei, chad gadya, chad gadya.

וְאָתָא נוּרָא וְשָׂרַף לְחוּטְרָא, דְּהִכָּה לְכַלְבָּא, דְּנָשַׁךְ לְשׁוּנְרָא, דְּאָכְלָה לְגַדְיָא, דְּזַבִּין אַבָּא בִּתְרֵי זוּזֵי, חַד גַּדְיָא, חַד גַּדְיָא

V'ata nura v'saraf l'chutra, d'hica l'calba, d'nashach l'shunra, d'achla l'gadya, d'zabin aba b'trei zuzei, chad gadya, chad gadya.

וְאָתָא מַיָּא וְכָבָה לְנוּרָא, דְּשָׂרַף לְחוּטְרָא, דְּהִכָּה לְכַלְבָּא, דְּנָשַׁךְ לְשׁוּנְרָא, דְּאָכְלָה לְגַדְיָא, דְּזַבִּין אַבָּא בִּתְרֵי זוּזֵי, חַד גַּדְיָא, חַד גַּדְיָא.

V'ata maya v'chaba l'nura, d'saraf l'chutra, d'hica l'calba, d'nashach l'shunra, d'achla l'gadya, d'zabin aba b'trei zuzei, chad gadya, chad gadya.

וְאָתָא תוֹרָא וְשָׁתָה לְמַיָּא, דְּכָבָה לְנוּרָא, דְּשָׂרַף לְחוּטְרָא, דְּהִכָּה לְכַלְבָּא, דְּנָשַׁךְ לְשׁוּנְרָא, דְּאָכְלָה לְגַדְיָא, דְּזַבִּין אַבָּא בִּתְרֵי זוּזֵי, חַד גַּדְיָא, חַד גַּדְיָא.

V'ata tora v'shata l'maya, d'chaba l'nura, d'saraf l'chutra, d'hica l'calba, d'nashach l'shunra, d'achla l'gadya, d'zabin aba b'trei zuzei, chad gadya, chad gadya.

וְאָתָא הַשּׁוֹחֵט וְשָׁחַט לְתוֹרָא, דְּשָׁתָה לְמַיָּא, דְּכָבָה לְנוּרָא, דְּשָׂרַף לְחוּטְרָא, דְּהִכָּה לְכַלְבָּא, דְּנָשַׁךְ לְשׁוּנְרָא, דְּאָכְלָה לְגַדְיָא, דְּזַבִּין אַבָּא בִּתְרֵי זוּזֵי, חַד גַּדְיָא, חַד גַּדְיָא.

V'ata hashochet v'shachat l'tora, d'shata l'maya, d'chaba l'nura, d'saraf l'chutra, d'hica l'calba, d'nashach l'shunra, d'achla l'gadya, d'zabin aba b'trei zuzei, chad gadya, chad gadya.

וְאָתָא מַלְאַךְ הַמָּוֶת וְשָׁחַט לְשׁוֹחֵט, דְּשָׁחַט לְתוֹרָא, דְּשָׁתָה לְמַיָּא, דְּכָבָה לְנוּרָא, דְּשָׂרַף לְחוּטְרָא, דְּהִכָּה לְכַלְבָּא, דְּנָשַׁךְ לְשׁוּנְרָא, דְּאָכְלָה לְגַדְיָא, דְּזַבִּין אַבָּא בִּתְרֵי זוּזֵי, חַד גַּדְיָא, חַד גַּדְיָא.

V'ata malach hamavet v'shachat l'shochet, d'shachat l'tora, d'shata l'maya, d'chaba l'nura, d'saraf l'chutra, d'hica l'calba, d'nashach l'shunra, d'achla l'gadya, d'zabin aba b'trei zuzei, chad gadya, chad gadya.

וְאָתָא הַקָּדוֹשׁ בָּרוּךְ הוּא וְשָׁחַט לְמַלְאַךְ הַמָּוֶת, דְּשָׁחַט לְשׁוֹחֵט, דְּשָׁחַט לְתוֹרָא, דְּשָׁתָה לְמַיָּא, דְּכָבָה לְנוּרָא, דְּשָׂרַף לְחוּטְרָא, דְּהִכָּה לְכַלְבָּא, דְּנָשַׁךְ לְשׁוּנְרָא, דְּאָכְלָה לְגַדְיָא דְּזַבִּין אַבָּא בִּתְרֵי זוּזֵי, חַד גַּדְיָא, חַד גַּדְיָא.

V'ata ha-Kadosh Baruch Hu, v'ishachat l'malach hamavet, d'shachat l'shochet, d'shachat l'tora, d'shata l'maya, d'chaba l'nura, d'saraf l'chutra, d'hica l'calba, d'nashach l'shunra, d'achla l'gadya, d'zabin aba b'trei zuzei, chad gadya, chad gadya.

One little goat, one little goat that father bought for two zuzim. One little goat, one little goat.

Along came a cat and ate the goat that father bought for two zuzim. One little goat, one little goat.

Along came a dog and bit the cat that ate the goat that father bought for two zuzim. One little goat, one little goat.

Along came a stick and hit the dog that bit the cat that ate the goat that father bought for two zuzim. One little goat, one little goat.

Along came a fire and burned the stick that hit the dog that bit the cat that ate the goat that father bought for two zuzim. One little goat, one little goat.

Along came some water and put out the fire that burned the stick that hit the dog that bit the cat that ate the goat that father bought for two zuzim. One little goat, one little goat.

Along came an ox and drank the water that put out the fire that burned the stick that hit the dog that bit the cat that ate the goat that father bought for two zuzim. One little goat, one little goat.

Along came a butcher and slaughtered the ox that drank the water that put out the fire that burned the stick that hit the dog that bit the cat that ate the goat that father bought for two zuzim. One little goat, one little goat.

Along came the angel of death and slaughtered the butcher who slaughtered the ox that drank the water that put out the fire that burned the stick that hit the dog that bit the cat that ate the goat that father bought for two zuzim. One little goat, one little goat.

Then along came the Holy One, Blessed be He, and slaughtered the angel of death who slaughtered the butcher who slaughtered the ox that drank the water that put out the fire that burned the stick that hit the dog that bit the cat that ate the goat that father bought for two zuzim. One little goat, one little goat.

Echad Mi Yodeya – Who Knows One?

אֶחָד מִי יוֹדֵעַ? אֶחָד אֲנִי יוֹדֵעַ. אֶחָד אֱלֹהֵינוּ שֶׁבַּשָּׁמַיִם וּבָאָרֶץ.

Echad mi yodea? Echad ani yodea. Echad Eloheinu she-bashamayim u'va'aretz.

שְׁנַיִם מִי יוֹדֵעַ? שְׁנַיִם אֲנִי יוֹדֵעַ. שְׁנֵי לוּחוֹת הַבְּרִית, אֶחָד אֱלֹהֵינוּ שֶׁבַּשָּׁמַיִם וּבָאָרֶץ.

Shnayim mi yodea? Shnayim ani yodea. Shnei luchot ha-brit, echad Eloheinu she-bashamayim u'va'aretz.

שְׁלֹשָׁה מִי יוֹדֵעַ? שְׁלֹשָׁה אֲנִי יוֹדֵעַ. שְׁלֹשָׁה אָבוֹת, שְׁנֵי לוּחוֹת הַבְּרִית, אֶחָד אֱלֹהֵינוּ שֶׁבַּשָּׁמַיִם וּבָאָרֶץ.

Shloshah mi yodea? Shloshah ani yodea. Shloshah avot, shnei luchot ha-brit, echad Eloheinu she-bashamayim u'va'aretz.

אַרְבַּע מִי יוֹדֵעַ? אַרְבַּע אֲנִי יוֹדֵעַ. אַרְבַּע אִמָּהוֹת, שְׁלֹשָׁה אָבוֹת, שְׁנֵי לוּחוֹת הַבְּרִית, אֶחָד אֱלֹהֵינוּ שֶׁבַּשָּׁמַיִם וּבָאָרֶץ.

Arbah mi yodea? Arbah ani yodea. Arbah imahot, shloshah avot, shnei luchot ha-brit, echad Eloheinu she-bashamayim u'va'aretz.

חֲמִשָּׁה מִי יוֹדֵעַ? חֲמִשָּׁה אֲנִי יוֹדֵעַ. חֲמִשָּׁה חֻמְשֵׁי תּוֹרָה, אַרְבַּע אִמָּהוֹת, שְׁלֹשָׁה אָבוֹת, שְׁנֵי לוּחוֹת הַבְּרִית, אֶחָד אֱלֹהֵינוּ שֶׁבַּשָּׁמַיִם וּבָאָרֶץ.

Chamishah mi yodea? Chamishah ani yodea. Chamishah chumshei Torah, arbah imahot, shloshah avot, shnei luchot ha-brit, echad Eloheinu she-bashamayim u'va'aretz.

שִׁשָּׁה מִי יוֹדֵעַ? שִׁשָּׁה אֲנִי יוֹדֵעַ. שִׁשָּׁה סִדְרֵי מִשְׁנָה, חֲמִשָּׁה חֻמְשֵׁי תּוֹרָה, אַרְבַּע אִמָּהוֹת, שְׁלֹשָׁה אָבוֹת שְׁנֵי לוּחוֹת הַבְּרִית, אֶחָד אֱלֹהֵינוּ שֶׁבַּשָּׁמַיִם וּבָאָרֶץ.

Shishah mi yodea? Shishah ani yodea. Shishah sidrei mishnah, chamishah chumshei Torah, arbah imahot, shloshah avot, shnei luchot ha-brit, echad Eloheinu she-bashamayim u'va'aretz.

שִׁבְעָה מִי יוֹדֵעַ? שִׁבְעָה אֲנִי יוֹדֵעַ. שִׁבְעָה יְמֵי שַׁבַּתָּא, שִׁשָּׁה סִדְרֵי מִשְׁנָה, חֲמִשָּׁה חֻמְשֵׁי תוֹרָה, אַרְבַּע אִמָּהוֹת, שְׁלֹשָׁה אָבוֹת, שְׁנֵי לוּחוֹת הַבְּרִית, אֶחָד אֱלֹהֵינוּ שֶׁבַּשָּׁמַיִם וּבָאָרֶץ.

שְׁמוֹנָה מִי יוֹדֵעַ? שְׁמוֹנָה אֲנִי יוֹדֵעַ. שְׁמוֹנָה יְמֵי מִילָה, שִׁבְעָה יְמֵי שַׁבַּתָּא, שִׁשָּׁה סִדְרֵי מִשְׁנָה, חֲמִשָּׁה חֻמְשֵׁי תוֹרָה, אַרְבַּע אִמָּהוֹת, שְׁלֹשָׁה אָבוֹת, שְׁנֵי לוּחוֹת הַבְּרִית, אֶחָד אֱלֹהֵינוּ שֶׁבַּשָּׁמַיִם וּבָאָרֶץ.

תִּשְׁעָה מִי יוֹדֵעַ? תִּשְׁעָה אֲנִי יוֹדֵעַ. תִּשְׁעָה יַרְחֵי לֵדָה, שְׁמוֹנָה יְמֵי מִילָה, שִׁבְעָה יְמֵי שַׁבַּתָּא, שִׁשָּׁה סִדְרֵי מִשְׁנָה, חֲמִשָּׁה חֻמְשֵׁי תוֹרָה, אַרְבַּע אִמָּהוֹת, שְׁלֹשָׁה אָבוֹת, שְׁנֵי לוּחוֹת הַבְּרִית, אֶחָד אֱלֹהֵינוּ שֶׁבַּשָּׁמַיִם וּבָאָרֶץ.

עֲשָׂרָה מִי יוֹדֵעַ? עֲשָׂרָה אֲנִי יוֹדֵעַ. עֲשָׂרָה דִבְּרַיָּא, תִּשְׁעָה יַרְחֵי לֵדָה, שְׁמוֹנָה יְמֵי מִילָה, שִׁבְעָה יְמֵי שַׁבַּתָּא, שִׁשָּׁה סִדְרֵי מִשְׁנָה, חֲמִשָּׁה חֻמְשֵׁי תוֹרָה, אַרְבַּע אִמָּהוֹת, שְׁלֹשָׁה אָבוֹת, שְׁנֵי לוּחוֹת הַבְּרִית, אֶחָד אֱלֹהֵינוּ שֶׁבַּשָּׁמַיִם וּבָאָרֶץ.

Shivah mi yodea? Shivah ani yodea. Shivah y'mei shabtah, shishah sidrei mishnah, chamishah chumshei Torah, arbah imahot, shloshah avot, shnei luchot ha-brit, echad Eloheinu she-bashamayim u'va'aretz.

Shmonah mi yodea? Shmonah ani yodea. Shmonah y'mei milah, shivah y'mei shabtah, shishah sidrei mishnah, chamishah chumshei Torah, arbah imahot, shloshah avot, shnei luchot ha-brit, echad Eloheinu she-bashamayim u'va'aretz.

Tishah mi yodea? Tishah ani yodea. Tishah yarchei leidah, shmonah y'mei milah, shivah y'mei shabtah, shishah sidrei mishnah, chamishah chumshei Torah, arbah imahot, shloshah avot, shnei luchot ha-brit, echad Eloheinu she-bashamayim u'va'aretz.

Asarah mi yodea? Asarah ani yodea. Asarah dibrayah, tishah yarchei leidah, shmonah y'mei milah, shivah y'mei shabtah, shishah sidrei mishnah, chamishah chumshei Torah, arbah imahot, shloshah avot, shnei luchot ha-brit, echad Eloheinu she-bashamayim u'va'aretz.

אַחַד עָשָׂר מִי יוֹדֵעַ? אַחַד עָשָׂר אֲנִי יוֹדֵעַ. אַחַד עָשָׂר כּוֹכְבַיָּא, עֲשָׂרָה דִבְּרַיָּא, תִּשְׁעָה יַרְחֵי לֵדָה, שְׁמוֹנָה יְמֵי מִילָה, שִׁבְעָה יְמֵי שַׁבַּתָּא, שִׁשָּׁה סִדְרֵי מִשְׁנָה, חֲמִשָּׁה חֻמְשֵׁי תוֹרָה, אַרְבַּע אִמָּהוֹת, שְׁלֹשָׁה אָבוֹת, שְׁנֵי לוּחוֹת הַבְּרִית, אֶחָד אֱלֹהֵינוּ שֶׁבַּשָּׁמַיִם וּבָאָרֶץ.

Achad-asar mi yodea? Achad-asar ani yodea. Achad-asar kochvayah, asarah dibrayah, tishah yarchei leidah, shmonah y'mei milah, shivah y'mei shabtah, shishah sidrei mishnah, chamishah chumshei Torah, arbah imahot, shloshah avot, shnei luchot ha-brit, echad Eloheinu she-bashamayim u'va'aretz.

שְׁנֵים עָשָׂר מִי יוֹדֵעַ? שְׁנֵים עָשָׂר אֲנִי יוֹדֵעַ. שְׁנֵים עָשָׂר שִׁבְטַיָּא, אַחַד עָשָׂר כּוֹכְבַיָּא, עֲשָׂרָה דִבְּרַיָּא, תִּשְׁעָה יַרְחֵי לֵדָה, שְׁמוֹנָה יְמֵי מִילָה, שִׁבְעָה יְמֵי שַׁבַּתָּא, שִׁשָּׁה סִדְרֵי מִשְׁנָה, חֲמִשָּׁה חֻמְשֵׁי תוֹרָה, אַרְבַּע אִמָּהוֹת, שְׁלֹשָׁה אָבוֹת, שְׁנֵי לוּחוֹת הַבְּרִית, אֶחָד אֱלֹהֵינוּ שֶׁבַּשָּׁמַיִם וּבָאָרֶץ.

Shneim-asar mi yodea? Shneim-asar ani yodea. Shneim-asar shivtayah, achad-asar kochvayah, asarah dibrayah, tishah yarchei leidah, shmonah y'mei milah, shivah y'mei shabtah, shishah sidrei mishnah, chamishah chumshei Torah, arbah imahot, shloshah avot, shnei luchot ha-brit, echad Eloheinu she-bashamayim u'va'aretz.

שְׁלֹשָׁה עָשָׂר מִי יוֹדֵעַ? שְׁלֹשָׁה עָשָׂר אֲנִי יוֹדֵעַ. שְׁלֹשָׁה עָשָׂר מִדַּיָּא, שְׁנֵים עָשָׂר שִׁבְטַיָּא, אַחַד עָשָׂר כּוֹכְבַיָּא, עֲשָׂרָה דִבְּרַיָּא, תִּשְׁעָה יַרְחֵי לֵדָה, שְׁמוֹנָה יְמֵי מִילָה, שִׁבְעָה יְמֵי שַׁבַּתָּא, שִׁשָּׁה סִדְרֵי מִשְׁנָה, חֲמִשָּׁה חֻמְשֵׁי תוֹרָה, אַרְבַּע אִמָּהוֹת, שְׁלֹשָׁה אָבוֹת, שְׁנֵי לוּחוֹת הַבְּרִית, אֶחָד אֱלֹהֵינוּ שֶׁבַּשָּׁמַיִם וּבָאָרֶץ.

Shloshah-asar mi yodea? Shloshah-asar ani yodea. Shloshah-asar midayah, shneim-asar shivtayah, achad-asar kochvayah, asarah dibrayah, tishah yarchei leidah, shmonah y'mei milah, shivah y'mei shabtah, shishah sidrei mishnah, chamishah chumshei Torah, arbah imahot, shloshah avot, shnei luchot ha-brit, echad Eloheinu she-bashamayim u'va'aretz.

Who knows one? I know one. One is our G-d in Heaven and Earth.

Who knows two? I know two. Two are the tablets of the covenant. One is our G-d in Heaven and Earth.

Who knows three? I know three. Three are the patriarchs. Two are the tablets of the covenant. One is our G-d in Heaven and Earth.

Who knows four? I know four. Four are the matriarchs. Three are the patriarchs. Two are the tablets of the covenant. One is our G-d in Heaven and Earth.

Who knows five? I know five. Five are the books of the Torah. Four are the matriarchs. Three are the patriarchs. Two are the tablets of the covenant. One is our G-d in Heaven and Earth.

Who knows six? I know six. Six are the orders of the Mishnah. Five are the books of the Torah. Four are the matriarchs. Three are the patriarchs. Two are the tablets of the covenant. One is our G-d in Heaven and Earth.

Who knows seven? I know seven. Seven are the days of the week. Six are the orders of the Mishnah. Five are the books of the Torah. Four are the matriarchs. Three are the patriarchs. Two are the tablets of the covenant. One is our G-d in Heaven and Earth

Who knows eight? I know eight. Eight are the days for circumcision. Seven are the days of the week. Six are the orders of the Mishnah. Five are the books of the Torah. Four are the matriarchs. Three are the patriarchs. Two are the tablets of the covenant. One is our G-d in Heaven and Earth.

Who knows nine? I know nine. Nine are the months of childbirth. Eight are the days for circumcision. Seven are the days of the week.

Six are the orders of the Mishnah. Five are the books of the Torah. Four are the matriarchs. Three are the patriarchs. Two are the tablets of the covenant. One is our G-d in Heaven and Earth.

Who knows ten? I know ten. Ten are the Words from Sinai. Nine are the months of childbirth. Eight are the days for circumcision. Seven are the days of the week. Six are the orders of the Mishnah. Five are the books of the Torah. Four are the matriarchs. Three are the patriarchs. Two are the tablets of the covenant. One is our G-d in Heaven and Earth.

Who knows eleven? I know eleven. Eleven are the stars. Ten are the Words from Sinai. Nine are the months of childbirth. Eight are the days for circumcision. Seven are the days of the week. Six are the orders of the Mishnah. Five are the books of the Torah. Four are the matriarchs. Three are the patriarchs. Two are the tablets of the covenant. One is our G-d in Heaven and Earth.

Who knows twelve? I know twelve. Twelve are the tribes. Eleven are the stars. Ten are the Words from Sinai. Nine are the months of childbirth. Eight are the days for circumcision. Seven are the days of the week. Six are the orders of the Mishnah. Five are the books of the Torah. Four are the matriarchs. Three are the patriarchs. Two are the tablets of the covenant. One is our G-d in Heaven and Earth.

Who knows thirteen? I know thirteen. Thirteen are the attributes of G-d. Twelve are the tribes. Eleven are the stars. Ten are the Words from Sinai. Nine are the months of childbirth. Eight are the days for circumcision. Seven are the days of the week. Six are the orders of the Mishnah. Five are the books of the Torah. Four are the matriarchs. Three are the patriarchs. Two are the tablets of the covenant. One is our G-d in Heaven and Earth.

Eliyahu Hanavi – The Prophet Elijah

אֵלִיָּהוּ הַנָּבִיא, אֵלִיָּהוּ הַתִּשְׁבִּי, אֵלִיָּהוּ הַגִּלְעָדִי, בִּמְהֵרָה יָבֹא אֵלֵינוּ עִם מָשִׁיחַ בֶּן דָּוִד.

Eliyahu ha-navi, Eliyahu ha-tishbi, Eliyahu ha-giladi. Bimheirah yavo eleynu, im Mashiach ben David.

May Elijah the prophet, Elijah the Tishbite, Elijah of Gilead, quickly in our day come to us heralding redemption with the Messiah, son of David.

Let My People Go

"When Israel was in Egypt land, let my people go.
Oppressed so hard they could not stand, let my people go."
Go down, Moses, way down in Egypt land.
Tell old Pharaoh, let my people go!

"Thus saith the Lord" bold Moses said, "Let my people go,
If not I'll smite your firstborn dead, let my people go."
Go down, Moses, way down in Egypt land.
Tell old Pharaoh, let my people go!

"No more shall they in bondage toil, let my people go.
Let them come out with Egypt's spoils, let my people go."
Go down, Moses, way down in Egypt land.
Tell old Pharaoh, let my people go!

"When people stop this slavery, let my people go.
Soon may all the earth be free, let my people go."
Go down, Moses, way down in Egypt land.
Tell old Pharaoh, let my people go!

www.ingramcontent.com/pod-product-compliance
Lightning Source LLC
Chambersburg PA
CBHW070129140326
41255CB00004B/607